THE PENGUIN CLASSICS

EDITED BY E.V. RIEU

L31

EURIPIDES

THREE PLAYS

HIPPOLYTUS

IPHIGENIA IN TAURIS

ALCESTIS

*

TRANSLATED BY PHILIP VELLACOTT

PENGUIN BOOKS

BALTIMORE · MARYLAND

Penguin Books Ltd, Harmondsworth, Middlesex

U.S.A.: Penguin Books Inc., 3300 Clipper Mill Road, Baltimore 11, Md

AUSTRALIA: Penguin Books Pty Ltd, 762 Whitehorse Road,
Mitcham, Victoria

—

First published 1953
Reprinted 1956, 1959

Made and printed in Great Britain
by The Whitefriars Press Ltd
London and Tonbridge

CONTENTS

*

TO
THE ATTIC PLAYERS

*

INTRODUCTION

I

EURIPIDES was born in 484 B.C. and died in 407. He was a Greek. He was also an Athenian, which means very much more; for what Greece was to the rest of the world, Athens was to the rest of Greece — 'the Hellas of Hellas'. The State of Athens consisted, at the beginning of the fifth century B.C., of some 10,000 adult male citizens with their dependants and slaves; its territory comprised the town of Athens, the harbour of Peiraeus, and the surrounding district known as Attica, in all about the area of a small English county. During the lifetime of Euripides this tiny nation not only gained and lost the political leadership of the Greek world, but contributed to European civilizations of the future an incalculable proportion of their thought and culture, and was foremost, unapproached by any rival in any field, in the creation of 'the glory that was Greece'.

In the meteoric rise of Athens to her unique position of leadership one day can be named as decisive: the day of the Battle of Salamis, 480 B.C. The invading army of Persia was in occupation of Athens; the greater part of the Athenian people had crossed by ship to the island of Salamis, from whose shores they watched their own fleet utterly rout the Persian fleet in a pitched battle in the strait. The Persian land force, deprived of its means of supply, had to fall back, to be defeated and cut to pieces the following year at Plataea. Their retreat left the Athenians with a devastated city, but in an unquestioned position as leaders of Greek independence; and this position they were destined to hold for nearly fifty years, the first fifty years of Euripides' life. In the Battle of Salamis Aeschylus, the first of the great tragedians, fought as a hoplite, or heavy-armed soldier; after the battle the young Sophocles danced in a procession of boys to celebrate the victory; so, inevitably, tradition stretched a point and remembered that Euripides had been born in Salamis, even on the very day of battle.

But the dozen years dividing Euripides from his predecessor in the poetic art were a watershed that turned the two streams towards different oceans. Sophocles was old enough to know that he belonged to the day of glory; with the eye of faith he saw in men the greatness that might be, in gods the majesty of 'old eternal justice', in Athens the inextinguishable flame of civic virtue and social wisdom, which gleamed even through the shadow of decadence and defeat. But by the time Euripides reached years of understanding the heroes of Salamis were middle-aged – probably the more middle-aged because heroic. In war-time – and hardly one of those years in Greece could be called peaceful – a new generation rises very quickly. When Sophocles was eighty and Euripides sixty-eight they still belonged to different generations, and their works reflect two different worlds of thought and interpretation of experience. 'To hold the gods in awe' is, for the younger poet, no longer a reliable rule for achieving happiness or avoiding disaster. He insists on asking, Which god? Aphrodite or Artemis? Sophrosyne ('Moderation') or Dionysus? He assumes that innocence is as likely to suffer as guilt; cruelty as likely to prosper as courage. A supernatural world there certainly is; but the forces governing its operation, its relation to our world, are unknowable and their results unpredictable. Orestes says of the gods, 'Their divine world is as chaotic as our mortal one'. Yet in the same decade, in the same city, in the same war, the Chorus in Sophocles' *King Oedipus* declare, 'All secrets of earth are known to Zeus and Apollo', and ask, 'Shall he by any armour be defended/From God's sharp wrath, who casts out right for wrong?' Euripides was a man of deep religious consciousness; but for him religious truth, in the words of Phaedra's Nurse, was 'hidden from us in clouds and darkness'. In that century as in ours the urgencies of war added vividness to both scepticism and belief.

Euripides was just over fifty when the war against Sparta began; he never again knew Athens at peace. What part, if any, he took in the war is not known; but the war, like every other manifestation of human pride, folly, cruelty and weakness, enters into his plays, sometimes as a major theme, as in *The Trojan Women* and *Andromache*, sometimes more quietly, as in the sad reminiscences of the Chorus in *Iphigenia in Tauris*. Before the war began he had already shown, in *Medea*, that he was working with a new conception of tragedy, one in which, as has sometimes been said, the central figure or tragic hero is not any individual, but humanity itself; in which wrongdoers and wronged alike are victims of cosmic forces – revenge, lust for power, sexual desire, the ecstasy of wild nature, pride, and yet again revenge. The long progress of the war, with its annual series of blunders, crimes and heroisms and its growing sense of no escape from an ordained sequence of catastrophes, must continually have impressed upon him this view of life, and its relation to his art. The day of Marathon and Salamis, the day of individuals, was past. The small city-state was now a nation and an empire, and prone to forget that it still incurred moral debts. Even in the three widely-differing plays selected for this volume it is evident that the main character-interest in no case centres round the person whose name gives the title to the play. What is studied is the impact of suffering not so much on an individual as on a group. Of this more must be said when we come to consider the plays themselves.

About the personal history of Euripides very little is known for certain. He belonged to a family of considerable rank. The legend (invented as a deadly slander) that his mother was a greengrocer, like the other legends of his hatred of women and his condonation of per-jury, merely illustrated the degree of dislike which so outspoken a critic of his own society might look to earn. A young man in his position would be expected to undertake numerous public duties, legal, administrative, political, and military, and to perfect his abilities as orator, diplomat, and soldier. In these respects Euripides was, as far as we know, not an ideal citizen. Such pursuits and interests demand, in greater or less degree, the 'unexamined' life, which for him was impossible. He is said to have had a great library; to have been a friend and pupil of the philosopher Anaxagoras, whose views on the material universe were in essence closely related to the atomic theories of modern science. He must certainly have sought the con-versation of women and of slaves in a way which would draw uneasy glances from other Athenians; and he must have hated and feared the conventions of organized society – the politeness and conformities which he saw so dangerously screwing down the safety-valve on the real and inescapable forces of life, the passions which are in human blood and will obey their own laws and no others – Aphrodite, Artemis, and Dionysus. Such a man was likely to win grudging admira-tion and little popularity. In the course of fifty years' writing of plays for the festivals of Dionysus he was awarded the prize only four or five times.

He must also have had some acquaintance with Socrates, who was about fifteen years his junior. There was much that they had in com-

mon. They were the two great questioners of their age; they both
believed passionately that the reality of the world is spiritual, not
material; that integrity of soul is worth more than any wealth.
Euripides, however, differed from Socrates in valuing human beings,
even when they were not intelligent. Socrates is said to have been a
keen attender at Euripides' plays, and to have walked out of the
theatre at a line he disagreed with. The fate which Euripides risked
for a generation and finally avoided by voluntary exile fell to Socrates
ten years later, when he was condemned to death for corrupting the
youth of Athens and teaching them not to believe in the city's gods.
Both were men dedicated to the work of probing common beliefs, of
exhibiting praised examples in a hard unflattering light, and of per-
suading men to look not to Olympus, but within themselves, for both
knowledge and the virtue to use it. But Euripides never figures in
Plato's Socratic dialogues, and there is little, if any, Socratic influence
recognizable in the plays. As Professor Gilbert Murray has said, 'It is
likely enough that both men were too vivid and original to be quite
comfortable in the same room.' Certainly the average Athenian citizen
could not feel comfortable with either of them.

Euripides' growing unpopularity seems to have come to a head in
some way, unknown to us, which made him decide to leave his home
for ever. It is difficult to exaggerate the painfulness which this decision
must have held for him, since to a Greek his city meant so much more
than our home town could ever mean to us – and Athens was the city
of cities. Euripides had more than once been invited by Archelaus,
King of Macedon, to live as a guest at his court. Though Greeks
affected to regard Macedonia as the fringe of barbarism – life in the
North undoubtedly had certain rugged, Homeric features – yet
Archelaus was a Greek whose intelligence and vitality had already
attracted various other notables, painters and poets, to accept similar
invitations. Euripides now went to Macedon and was welcomed.
There he could enjoy at the same time the personal luxury of generous
hospitality and the wild grandeur of the Macedonian mountains. In
this exile, free at last – and just in time – from the weary, war-ridden,
disillusioned world of Southern Greece, from a culture that was bent
on blinding its own eyes and cutting its own throat, Euripides in the
last year or two of his life produced what many will always regard as
his greatest work, *The Bacchae*. When the news of his death reached

Athens in 407, three years before the end of the war, Sophocles, now over ninety, appeared publicly in mourning for him.

II

Much argument has been spent to decide what sort of thinker Euripides was, and perhaps even more to exalt or condemn him as a dramatist. He has been called atheist and religious reformer, rationalist and irrationalist, prophet and platitudinarian. His writings have been ridiculed, damned with faint praise, explained, apologized for, and read more widely than the work of most of his contemporaries. To the bewilderment of our own age he makes a special appeal. His thought was agnostic, pessimist, and, above all, humanitarian. Discussion of his dramatic art must here be confined in the main to what can be illustrated from the three plays here translated, which cover fairly well the width of his range from tragedy to comedy, and do justice alike to his satire, pathos, and poetry.

His contemporary, Aristophanes, the writer of comedies, called him an atheist. It is true that he presents various gods on the stage in compromising situations, behaving a shade worse than mortals, envious and unscrupulous, lacking both dignity and humour. The prologues to *Hippolytus* and *Alcestis* both illustrate this. Death and Apollo haggle over souls like boys swopping stamps; Aphrodite makes it clear that she will cause two deaths out of pure pique, while Artemis in the epilogue comforts the dying victim with the promise that she will commit another useless slaughter to avenge him. The whole story of Iphigenia is presented as a test case for Apollo's reliability, and when at the last moment Apollo fails to help, it is Athene who appears to make his explanations, quite unconvincingly. (Exactly the same thing happens in another play, *Ion.*) These gods, in fact, are for Euripides no more than dramatic fictions.

That is not, however, to say that Euripides denied the existence of the gods. Professor Kitto, in his *Greek Tragedy*, has put the matter very clearly: 'The Greeks did not progress from taking their gods seriously to disbelieving in them or laughing at them. They did both (on suitable occasions) in every century from Homer to Aristotle.' Though Euripides has sometimes been presented as the unbeliever boldly shattering the credulity of the innocent, the probability is that a very large number of his fellow-citizens had discarded not only the

belief in such deities as Apollo and Aphrodite, but with it all sense
of anything superhuman and supernatural in the universe. This was
the folly, the *hybris* (arrogance), against which Euripides warns his
audience in half a dozen surviving tragedies. The world holds, or
human nature holds, impersonal forces of terrifying power which,
once set in motion, can cause unlimited suffering to guilty and
innocent, to individuals and communities alike. Such forces are represented by the figures of Aphrodite and Artemis. 'Aphrodite is no goddess!' exclaims the Nurse in *Hippolytus;* then, frightened at her own
blasphemy, but dimly seeing the truth that inspired it, 'She is something more than a goddess, something greater!' Similarly Apollo, the
most frequent object of attack or exposure by Euripides, represents
perhaps the determination of mortals to find divine sanction for their
own deeds. It is noticeable, however, that Zeus, the Father of gods
and men, is never treated by Euripides in this way, never shown on
the stage or called in question for what he has done (though legend
gave him a record hardly better than Apollo's). The nature of his
character and his being is called mysterious and unknowable; but
Zeus himself is always there, the given, unquestioned Divinity behind
every manifestation, the Unity of the supernatural world. In this
Euripides continued the monotheist tendency of poets and philo-
sophers who had preceded him, but always as a poet rather than as a
philosopher. That is to say, he propounds no system, states no dogma;
he does not strive to be consistent. A fragment shows us his general
agnosticism: 'He that pretends to have knowledge concerning the
gods has in truth no higher science than to persuade men by assertion.' The final chorus in *Alcestis* shows us his fatalism: 'There is no
remedy against Necessity.' And Hippolytus' slave puts it another way:
'Gods ought to be wiser than men' – the tragedy is that they are not.
They are amoral, impersonal, unfeeling, as Hippolytus in the end
finds out for himself. In other words, man, in the full range of his
capacity for goodness, for suffering and sympathy, is a creature on a
higher spiritual level than the universe in which he is set to live. The
compensations nature offers us for the affront of her blind and tyran-
nical power are the tenderness of human love, and the illimitable and
ever-inspiring beauty of earth, sea, and sky.

This quality of Euripides' thought strongly suggests comparison
with a modern English writer. Like Thomas Hardy, Euripides seems

to have been a man of deeply religious nature who longed for and
would have found a religion to satisfy his soul, if his devotion to truth
had allowed him to accept any of those answers to life's mysteries
that the contemporary world offered him. 'Necessity' and similar
abstractions offer no anchorage for faith, no motive or vindication of
goodness. Yet Euripides' work, like Hardy's, even in the very ruth-
lessness of its human portraiture, carries a passionate assertion of the
beauty and truth of goodness. But it does more: with a touching
restraint and subtlety it illuminates the moral issue in a constant series
of unexpected, simple, almost trivial situations; in every kind of
scene, ironic, melodramatic, comic, or tragic, he shows the true
worth of the quiet virtues, of modesty, dignity, kindness, and integrity,
and with it the partial and relative nature of most human achievement
of virtue. We see this in the attitude of the dying Hippolytus to his
father – sympathy for his sufferings, readiness to forgive; behaviour
which cannot but remind us, though Euripides makes no comment,
how earlier in the play Hippolytus has shown himself incapable of
similar nobility towards a woman. Another example is the gentleness
with which Euripides allows Iphigenia's selfish appeal to the Chorus
for help to be rebuked by the memory of the Chorus's own protest –
which earlier in the play Iphigenia had ignored – 'And what of us?
We have lost parents too. Where are they now?' There is the mingled
honesty, modesty, and devotion of the slave in the opening scene of
Hippolytus; and in *Alcestis* there is the surprising abstention of the
Pheraean elders from any comment whatever on Admetus' conduct,
when Pheres goes out, pursued by his son's curse, after the quarrel
over the coffin. Euripides presents the achievement or the failure of
goodness in those subtle, incidental forms in which it chiefly makes
or mars the life of ordinary people; but such achievement, whether
trivial or heroic, is not the gift of the gods, neither is it their concern
to reward it.

What, then, is the source of goodness? For Euripides, neither
divine sanction, nor, as Socrates held, human instruction. It was in
the first place 'nature', 'natural disposition', 'heredity'; and the
secondary advantage of a good upbringing was probably necessary as
well. Inevitably the source of evil was the same: human wickedness
he saw as indestructible and rooted in heredity, which, for Euripides
as for Ibsen, takes the place of the Aeschylean Ancestral Curse. This

thought is emphasized both by Phaedra and Theseus in *Hippolytus*. Upbringing may help to control inherited evil, but the intellect alone is powerless against it. *Hippolytus* is one of several tragedies in which Euripides shows the victory of irrational impulse over reason in a noble but unstable character; and the figure of Orestes in *Iphigenia in Tauris* suggests the same situation. In such mysterious conflicts, akin to madness, Euripides found the source of the deepest sorrows of humanity.

Like Hardy again, and for some of the same reasons, Euripides was attacked and hated by his contemporaries for the kind of subject he chose and for his treatment of themes which the conventional would prefer to avoid. Some of the commentaries still in use in English schools (written by contemporaries of Hardy) censure Euripides in prim terms for his 'errors of taste' in presenting on the stage women jealously or hopelessly in love with men, or sufferers doubting the usefulness of their appeals to the gods. Athenians of the fifth century B.C., like English society of the 'eighties, had a bad conscience about women, and Euripides rubbed salt on the sore. They knew the standard of morality was low, but they would not have male responsibility for it openly illustrated. Similarly, they knew that few of themselves believed in the gods in any religious sense; but, like their counterparts of to-day, they expected something quite different from official sources on public religious occasions such as the performances of plays – in fact, a vicarious piety. Openly expressed doubts as to the existence or power of gods interfered with too many useful sanctions and was intolerable bad form. They would pay a sophist to show them how to cheat in a law-court; but they were indignant when Hippolytus in a moment of rage shouted, 'My tongue swore: the oath does not bind my heart', even though before the play was over he had gone to his death rather than break his oath. The men and women of these plays made the fifth-century Athenians angry because they spoke the same language and thought in similar terms; and sometimes Euripides lets it be plainly seen that he is less interested in the person he is presenting (Phaedra, after all, lived in a remote and legendary age) than in the situation, which might occur any day in any street in Athens. This emphasis, indeed, is part of Euripides' whole conception of tragedy, which we shall consider later in looking more closely at *Hippolytus*.

There are other significant points of contact between Euripides and Thomas Hardy. They accept the same quiet and courageous despair, a pessimism which believes that the universe is not on the side of goodness, that whatever cosmic forces may exist are at best neutral, often capriciously cruel. They possess the same heroic perception, which they exemplify in simple and modest characters, that man's – and still more woman's – highest genius lies in suffering rather than in action; and that the beauty of pain nobly borne outweighs the deformity of a soulless world. They show the same sensitiveness to the infinite variety of loveliness in Nature. They betray the same tendency to sacrifice perfection of form to incisiveness of statement. For those at least who believe that Hardy, as a poetic and philosophic commentator on human life, is among the rare immortals of modern times, these comparisons may prove a help in the discovery, even through a translation, of the profundity and the humanity of Euripides.

Of Aeschylus' plays seven survive, of Sophocles' seven; of Euripides' nineteen. Aeschylus and Sophocles were honoured citizens till the day of their death; Euripides was driven by the hostility of his country-men to go into exile when over seventy years old. He was the one whose meaning, if not his art, was best understood; who was best hated and best loved. The love he earned was due very largely to the immense poetic appeal of his lyric writing. In the three plays included in this volume the most frequent source of his poetic inspiration is to be found in a love of Nature which was as penetrating and as universal as his love of humanity. His choruses are full of unforgettable landscapes: the shapely laurel and silver-green olive of Delos, the swan on the round lake where slow pools turn; the myriad whiteness of sea-birds on an island beach; the lost waters of Eridanus flowing down to an unknown sea; the quiet garden by the Western ocean where the daughters of evening sing under the golden apple-boughs; the lonely halcyon haunting the sharp sea-cliffs; the steep winding pastures, and dappled fawns stepping slender-footed from the high shady fir-trees. Then, he can paint the simple pleasures of life, whether social or solitary – here with a nostalgic shadow: 'The wed-dings in noble houses, the whirl of dancing, the bridesmaids singing together.' Still nearer to the experienced heart is his recognition of accepted despair, of the pain that cannot be escaped:

Not by weeping will you raise the dead to life.
        Sons of gods immortal
        Wither into darkness.

And,

Change follows change; Fate purposeless and blind
Uproots us from familiar soil:
        The longest life can find
        No rest from travel and toil.

If the modern producer of a Greek play finds the choral odes an em-
barrassment which he is tempted to mitigate by cuts, something is
wrong somewhere. In their own century they were remembered,
recited, thought over, and loved as an essential part of the play.

III

HIPPOLYTUS

Only one of Euripides' tragedies appears in this volume, *Hippolytus*.
It is usually a favourite play with modern readers; the subject is one
of absorbing human interest, while the dramatic power of the dialogue
shows Euripides at his best. Yet it does not conform to the usually
accepted tragic pattern; indeed, the analysis of the play's construction
presents certain features (which occur in a much more pronounced
form in other tragedies of Euripides) which have caused critics to
excuse, censure, and even abuse him as a dramatist.

The accepted form of a tragedy may be taken to be that described
by Aristotle in his *Poetics;* and Aristotle based his remarks mainly on
the work of Sophocles, and on *King Oedipus* in particular. A play of
this type has a central figure, who must be a person of some distinction and nobility, yet a person endowed with human qualities, perhaps weaknesses, which appeal to the audience as showing that he is
of the same flesh and blood as they. The character of this central figure
is subjected to an ordeal resulting from the combination of circumstances (which must not be strained or improbable) with some defect
or excess inherent in its own composition. There follows a revelation,
embodied in some dramatic act, of the fundamental goodness or bad-
ness of that character (in Shakespearean tragedy it is often a development as well as a revelation); and this act leads to a catastrophe,
either utter downfall or death, which is at the same time a statement

of the character's moral relation to the universe, a measuring of its chances against Necessity, and a claiming of sublimity in despair. Interest throughout is centred on the 'tragic hero'; the 'tragic agent' — the direct cause of the ordeal — may be the hero himself or some other person; the action illustrates the inevitable working of Fate in an ultimately just universe; and the audience (each one saying to himself, 'There, but for the grace of God, go I') are moved with a purifying pity for the fallen and a humbling sense of the greatness of the gods.

This dramatic pattern, far from being a Greek monopoly, is of course familiar in such plays as Shakespeare's *Macbeth* or Galsworthy's *Loyalties*. Other tragedies of Shakespeare show some of the traditional tragic elements with variations such as the 'redemption through suffering' theme at the end of *King Lear*. In every case the dramatic unity is provided by the 'tragic hero', who remains the centre of interest and earns from the audience both sympathy and censure, the former outweighing the latter. The satisfying rightness of such a pattern is self-evident.

Now what of *Hippolytus?* Hardly any of the pattern fits. Hippolytus himself wins much less of our sympathy than Phaedra. There is no revelation of his character as the action proceeds; even Phaedra's death hardly seems to affect him, while the obvious flaw in his character, his priggishness, though it appears as the cause of his death, because he would not break his oath of silence, does not in that instance invite any disapproval, but rather admiration. He is certainly not the centre of interest in the first half of the play, and in the second he shares the tragedy with Theseus. Then, the main action is a play within a play, and the 'tragic agent' is relegated to a prologue, where Aphrodite spoils all possibility of surprise in the development by telling us exactly what is to happen. Besides all this, there is the apparent falling apart of the plot immediately after Phaedra's death; the law-court flavour of Theseus' and Hippolytus' speeches; and the aloof objectivity of the Chorus in face of the deaths of Phaedra and Hippolytus, both which events they sadly but calmly accept even before they have occurred. Yet in spite of these unorthodoxies *Hippolytus* (and other similarly disconcerting plays such as *Medea*, *The Trojan Women*, *Andromache*) are, above all, good theatre, and for those who have once met them in the theatre have a lasting fascination.

Let us begin our view of the play by telling in simple words the old story that Euripides has used. Hippolytus was a noble young man vowed to chastity. Phaedra, his father's young wife, fell in love with him; he rejected her. Phaedra in passionate despair killed herself, and left an accusing letter. Theseus read the letter and hurled against Hippolytus a curse which was immediately fulfilled.

Euripides first wrote this play in a form different from that which has survived. This first draft presented Phaedra as a scheming and lecherous woman – the 'tragic agent' – while Hippolytus' role as 'tragic hero' was unchallenged. Such a treatment did not satisfy Euripides, and within a short time he re-wrote the play in the form we now have. The new form was called his 'recantation', and various fanciful motives for the change were attributed to him; but a general view of Euripides' work shows where his dissatisfaction lay. When he looked again at the 'tale of ancient wrong' he observed three things: first, that as usual the woman's side of the case had never been given a fair showing; secondly, that Hippolytus' attitude was as dangerous an offence against Nature as Phaedra's desire was against morality; thirdly, that Theseus was at least as much a victim of circumstance as the other two, and that he must share fully in the catastrophe. These three perceptions are characteristic of Euripides and can be seen to have guided his treatment of material in a number of other plays. The philosophy of life on which they are based asserts that happiness and suffering alike are indivisible; that their impact on the group is more significant than their impact on the individual, and the true 'tragic hero' is humanity; that evil, by the time its activity has gained any noticeable power, is already outside the control of any human agent, is something impersonal, something at the same time sub-human and super-human; in fact, something like one of the Olympian gods.

So, in our version of *Hippolytus*, the 'tragic agent' is divine, and the human characters are all primarily the innocent victims of Aphrodite. The question of their guilt is secondary. The meaning of Phaedra's words spoken as the Nurse goes out promising to 'find a medicine' for her is purposely left ambiguous. The guilt of her lying letter is plain enough – but who will judge harshly a woman driven to suicide by mental agony? Hippolytus' pride, his unfeeling words to Phaedra, the rash and obstinate fury of Theseus – these various offences are pointed out to us (the last of them by Artemis herself, most unctuously), but we do not accept them as accounting for the tragedy. In both guilt and innocence Phaedra, Hippolytus, and Theseus share alike; no one of them is pre-eminently either agent or victim. What we are shown is the impersonal power of the cosmic force represented by Aphrodite descending upon a closely-linked group of people and bringing them to comprehensive disaster. If there is a lesson to be drawn, it is that in a world containing incalculable forces, both of good and evil, a man can hope to preserve happiness only by the utmost care, humility, patience, and charitableness.

This view of the play points clearly to the unity which underlies its threefold division into prologue-epilogue, the story of Phaedra, and the story of Hippolytus. Euripides in various plays dealt with some of the impersonal and irresistible forces which he saw to be active in human communities: in *The Bacchae*, the primitive desire for oneness with Nature; in *The Trojan Women*, war; in *Medea*, revenge; in *Andromache*, political intrigue; in *Hippolytus*, sexual love. Aphrodite's opening words state the theme: 'Powerful among mortals.' That the effect of her power may be cruel as well as sweet is neither here nor there: Aphrodite is a fact of human nature and human society, and Phaedra's momentary vacillation, Hippolytus' flouting of natural impulse, Theseus' maddening jealousy, are all understandable errors fraught with infinite danger. In face of such danger, the Chorus in their last Ode disavow any desire to be heroic, and ask only for quietness and the gift of adapting principle to daily needs. The same attitude is earnestly recommended by the two representatives of the ordinary person, the Nurse and Hippolytus' servant. Such capitulation is apparently impossible for noble minds: they ram the rock and are sunk. What then is the solution? No solution is given. Euripides' outlook is admittedly pessimistic. Goodness and kindness and tolerance are right and to be pursued at all costs by those who will; but the universe is not on the side of goodness. It is not on any side at all; but hostility to human endeavour is its most noticeable feature.

IPHIGENIA IN TAURIS

This lively and curiously puzzling play is usually classed among Euripides' melodramas. It is primarily an adventure story in a remote and romantic setting, providing the familiar elements of suspense, violence, loyalty, intrigue; and its first aim seems to be entertainment. The happy ending – the distress and humiliation of a barbarian king would leave Athenian withers unwrung – helps to confirm this impression and send away the audience unconscious of tragedy or questioning. Those, however, whose minds return to look again find more matter for enquiry than appeared at first sight.

To begin with, although the scene is far from Troy and Argos, by the all-cleansing sea, the story is still that of the curse-ridden, blood-reeking house of Atreus. The whole action is concerned with the two chief surviving members of that house, two lives both blasted by inherited guilt, Iphigenia remembering her father as her murderer, Orestes remembering how he murdered his mother; both embittered against Fate and the gods; retaining the features of nobility, but driven near the end of endurance, the one by madness, the other by hope deferred. Agamemnon at Aulis had stained the altar of Artemis with blood: his son makes atonement for him when he stands bound before a blood-stained altar. Even if the ending is happy, this cannot be called a happy play. The brief joy of recognition is mingled with horrified revelations and soon ended by renewed suspense. What other threads of meaning, then, can be followed through this exciting tangle?

First, plainly, there is the part played by Apollo. Orestes in his first appearance challenges Apollo to show now or never the reliability of divine help and guidance for a man in extremity of need. Later, standing with Pylades before the altar, he says, 'I put no more faith in any words of Apollo'. After the recognition he says to his sister, 'I begin to see Apollo's purpose – I think we shall reach home!' Finally, when Apollo has failed to save the fugitives from capture, it is not he, and not Artemis, who steps in to put matters right, but Athene, whose only possible connexion with the affair is to speak as the representative of author or audience or both.

Now the argument to be drawn from this is not, I think, that Euripides is deriding his fellow-Athenians' belief in Apollo. The oracle and the whole institution at Delphi had made itself unpopular enough by its anti-Athenian attitude in the Peloponnesian War, and there was little serious religious belief to deride – indeed, the last choral Ode is rather like an invitation to join in amused mockery of a discredited god. What is suggested by this train of thought is surely the alternative, realistic ending to this grim story: one of stark tragedy, the capture and execution of Orestes, Iphigenia, and Pylades with their whole crew of Greek sailors and the women of the Chorus

as well. Too horrible an ending for Euripides' mood at the time he
wrote the play; but one in undoubted accord with the history of
Orestes' family, and perhaps providing the only satisfactory end to the
life of Orestes himself, poisoned, perverted, and broken as it had been
by his obedience to divine command; while the implication of his
innocent friends in wholesale disaster would provide but one more
example of what all Euripides' tragedies insist on, that such is usually
the way of things in a universe where justice is accidental and innocence no protection. At any rate, I think it is true to say that for the
reflective member of the audience this shadow hovers at the end of
the play, and Athene's smooth phrases have a designedly false ring.

   In the second place, though it is true that we should not regard
Euripides' criticism of Apollo as the attack of a rationalist minority
on a generally accepted faith, yet it may well be his censure of a
nearly universal superstition for which his countrymen had paid
dearly in very recent years. The Syracusan expedition of 415–13, a
shattering disaster from which Athens never recovered, had shown,
from the initial auguries and the mutilation of the Hermae right
through to the last fatal delay of Nicias, how the Athenian people
had failed in practice to outgrow the superstition which theoretically
they had dismissed. Surely it was the realization of this weakness that
made Euripides include in his play such passages as Orestes' outburst,
'Why, of course dreams mean nothing!' (lines 570–3) and Iphigenia's
declaration of belief that no god can be evil (lines 380–91); while
the simple rationalism of the herdsman (lines 291–4) is pointed by the
contrast between the plain sense of the savage and the insanity or
neurosis of the Greek. Moreover, three times in the play a sincere
prayer is uttered in the extremity of need, by Orestes (lines 77 ff.), by
Iphigenia (lines 1230 ff.) and again by Iphigenia reported in the
Messenger's speech (lines 1398 ff.); and not one of these prayers
wins the slightest response. Such hints, woven into the texture of the
play at many points, while they do not constitute the main theme or
purpose of the author, are nevertheless shadows which give a sombre-
ness to the whole action.

ALCESTIS

This is a play hard to classify by any Greek standard. Though it fits
well enough our broad modern sense of 'comedy', it has nothing

whatever in common with what the Athenian audience understood by
that word, beyond the fact that in one scene a demi-god, Heracles, is
presented as a roystering glutton. For the space of, perhaps, some
sixty lines the feeling has some affinity to that of the one 'satyric'
play that has survived complete, Euripides' *Cyclops*. The similarity,
however, is only partial and soon vanishes. The drunken speech of
Heracles, it is true, is pure comedy in itself; there is laughter, too,
in the description of him given by the servant who opens the scene – a
description punctuated by notes of carousal from off-stage; but all
laughter is suddenly hushed as the servant continues, 'And Alcestis
has gone; and I could not follow her body, or hold out my hand to say
good-bye'; and however much we may enjoy Heracles' rhapsody on
the pleasures of Aphrodite, the servant in his honest grief stands there
throughout, holding ribaldry in firm reins until the moment of
Heracles' supreme effort of self-recovery. As for the rest of the play,
much is written in the full tragic vein; and there is much of the
satire on human types and behaviour which appears again in the
tragedy of *Andromache* and the melodrama of *Ion*.

Something must be said of the celebrated essay on *Alcestis* which
formed the main part of A. W. Verrall's best-known book, *Euripides
the Rationalist*. Verrall's theories about the plays of Euripides are now
largely discredited; but it should not be forgotten that the general
attitude to Euripides which Verrall so zestfully combatted (an attitude
embodied in various seventy-year-old editions still in use in schools) –
this unimaginative attitude of patronizing apology is now even more
discredited; and it was Verrall who first entered a strong plea for
approaching Euripides' plays as the work of an intelligent thinker and
a competent artist. Unfortunately Verrall's enthusiasm for his author,
and the part he believed him to have played, led him to see evidence
in the most flimsy hints, and to credit the Athenian audience with
superhuman acumen. Euripides, too, has left some of his plays littered
with loose ends which invite conjecture; for example, the question
of the manner of Alcestis' burial. Verrall held that Euripides intended
it to be clear to the audience that the death of Alcestis was not death
at all, but a condition of unconsciousness induced by the superstitious
conviction that she was fated to die on that day; that Heracles, with
extraordinary perception, and in spite of being drunk, tumbled to the
truth, and eventually revived Alcestis and led her back to her home.

One of the chief evidences for this theory is the apparent speed with which Admetus buried his wife — within an hour or two of death. This arrangement, however, would be necessitated by any stage version of the story; to imply the passage of some days during a choral Ode, merely for the sake of realism, would have seemed quite unnecessary to any Greek dramatist. Another assumption essential to this theory is that Heracles was a man of subtle perception; and this is the one quality we cannot believe he possessed.

We may take it, then, that the story of the play is to be accepted simply as it stands. Even so, there are many fascinating questions which may not worry the reader, but will certainly present themselves to the producer and the actor. What does Euripides mean to imply was the personal relationship between Admetus and his wife before, during, and after these events? In speaking to her husband, Alcestis never once uses the word 'dear'. But though the title is *Alcestis*, the figure of chief interest is surely Admetus. Euripides presents him as the man of unheroic character and obvious faults, who, by some indefinable quality of charm, wins and holds the devotion of the most diverse types of people. The cold, remote Alcestis who honours her husband because it is in her bond to do so, cannot after all be dying for him out of sheer unmixed pride, for she does not speak like a fool. The tough and bluff Heracles undertakes the most daunting task of his adventurous life to help his timid, sensitive, self-pitying friend. The Chorus, who know all the circumstances, speak with unvarying sympathy and respect, even while they appeal for moderation, both of grief and of anger. Apollo, a god in disguise, feels so warm an admiration for the young king that he secures for him an exceptional favour from the Fates. The only one who appears to be proof against Admetus' charm is the servant, who remembers only his master's hot temper and heavy hand. Perhaps it is this same charm which makes all the male characters except the servant, including the Chorus, bestow all their sympathy upon Admetus for his bereavement, while only the female servant expresses pity for Alcestis: an excellent instance of Euripides' gentler kind of satire. He points a sterner finger when the two men pursue their wordy quarrel while Alcestis lies between them quiet in her coffin (just as in *Andromache* Peleus and Menelaus exchange abuse for a quarter of an hour while Andromache patiently kneels with bound hands). And after the satire and the sorrow, the play – almost alone in extant Greek drama – ends with a firm and humble hope that the future will be happier than the past. Alcestis is the earliest (apart from *Rhesus* and *Cyclops*) of Euripides' surviving plays; but it is not a young man's work – he was forty-six when it was produced. The gleam of hopefulness faded soon after: the next of his plays known to us is *Medea*.

*

In the translation I have used prose to represent the ordinary iambic line which is the common metre of dialogue; and verse for all the various, less regular, lyric metres. Sometimes (as at the first entrance of Alcestis and Admetus) a dialogue occurs in which one speaker uses iambic and the other lyric metre; here prose and verse make the distinction clear. In the verse passages I have used rhyme as a purely incidental ornament, adding to the words the same kind of extra discipline, which in Greek is provided by the exactness of the metrical rules. In the set choral odes I have marked the division into first and second strophe and antistrophe. In the original each antistrophe shows an exact metrical correspondence with the strophe, syllable by syllable, and sometimes there are clear patterns of thought or feeling woven across the metrical texture; and a producer will want to know where the divisions come, even though in a translation faithfulness must often preclude more than a limited degree of metrical correspondence. The second strophe and antistrophe are generally built on a different set of metrical units from that used in the first; this change I have indicated sometimes by a change from rhymed to unrhymed lines, or vice versa, always by a change of rhythm. Only occasionally (as in *Hippolytus*, p. 44, 'You are beside the door', etc.) have I attempted to use in English anything like the same metre as that used in the Greek, for the simple reason that the same metre may have an entirely different emotional effect in the two languages. In general, I have eschewed archaic diction. Though it is quite true that Euripides and all the tragedians used it in every play, yet I am convinced that it cannot have produced upon the minds of the Athenian audience the immediate torpor of unreality which pastiche Jacobean produces upon us to-day. I have aimed at making the translation, wherever possible, exact; that is to say, I have tried to represent faithfully, by one device or another, every idea, image, and association expressed in the poet's original words.

The aspects of Euripides' thought and work which I have touched upon in this Introduction are of necessity limited by the fact that only three of his nineteen extant plays are here presented. Some reference to other plays has obviously been necessary, but in general I have tried to limit this account to what can fairly be illustrated from these three. For the general reader there is not a wide choice of books about Euripides; two, I think, will give almost everything that is needed. Professor Gilbert Murray's *Euripides and His Age* is a fascinating and stimulating study covering the whole ground; while for those with a more exact interest in the literary criticism of the plays, and the relation of Euripides' work to that of the other Greek dramatists, there is no more penetrating and illuminating book than Professor H. D. F. Kitto's *Greek Tragedy*, in particular those chapters relating to Euripides.

To those who are moved to attempt the production of these plays I would appeal primarily to treat the text in a straightforward manner, to avoid anything like a 'period' flavour, or any undue solemnity; not to be afraid – at least in *Iphigenia* and *Alcestis* – of getting a laugh here and there. In most cases (I am thinking of amateur productions) I believe three to be the ideal number for the Chorus; and the lines of the Chorus, whether dialogue or lyric, should be suitably divided among the three and spoken *solo*, unison speaking being reserved for very occasional short passages, such as the prayer, 'Apollo, Lord of Healing', in *Alcestis*. The singing of lyric passages is almost always a mistake, because the words are meant to be heard and understood. An open stage without any curtain, showing a scene which is illuminated as the house-lights go down, is a help in establishing that close contact between actors and spectators, which was a feature of the original observance. A stage with front steps leading to the auditorium, or with extensions to right and left in front of the proscenium, makes the handling of the Chorus much easier. The plays should, of course, be produced without any interval; but unfortunately this is so unpopular with audiences that it is worth while to find some way of interrupting the action; and the continuity can sometimes be partly restored by beginning the second half with a repetition of the grouping or tableau with which the first half ended.   P. H. V.

HIPPOLYTUS

*

Characters in order of appearance:

APHRODITE, *the Goddess of Sexual Love*
HIPPOLYTUS, *bastard son of Theseus*
CHORUS *of Huntsmen attending Hippolytus*
SERVANT *of Hippolytus*
CHORUS *of Women of Troezen*
NURSE *attending Phaedra*
PHAEDRA, *wife of Theseus*
THESEUS, *King of Athens and Troezen*
MESSENGER
ARTEMIS, *the huntress Goddess of Virginity*

*

The scene is before the royal palace at Troezen, where Theseus is spending a year of voluntary exile to atone for bloodshed. On one side of the stage is a statue of APHRODITE, *on the other a statue of* ARTEMIS. *In the centre is the door of the palace.*

Enter APHRODITE.

APHRODITE: Powerful among mortals, glorious among the
  gods,
I am Aphrodite, named in heaven The Cyprian.
On earth, from the Eastern shore to the outward ocean of
  the West,
Over all that see the light of the sun my rule extends.
To those who reverence my powers I shew favour,
And throw to the earth those I find arrogant and proud.
For gods too have their pride; and it is their nature
To enjoy receiving honour from the mortal race.
And that my words are true I shall show this very day.
Hippolytus, the son whom the Amazon bore to Theseus,
Who was trained from a child by Pittheus the Severe, —

Hippolytus, alone among the inhabitants of Troezen,
Calls me the most pernicious of the heavenly powers;
He abhors the bed of love; marriage he renounces;
Honours Apollo's sister, Artemis daughter of Zeus.
All day with her, the virgin, he ranges the green woods,
With his swift hounds emptying the earth of beasts,
Too fond of company too high for mortal men.
I do not envy them their sport – I have little cause;
But Hippolytus has insulted me and shall suffer for it
This very day. My plans, long laid, are well begun,
And little work remains.

                              Two years ago Hippolytus
Left Pittheus' house for Athens, the city of Pandion,
To attend the holy Mysteries and complete his initiation;
And there the noble Phaedra saw him, his father's wife, –
And a terrible lust, by my contrivance, captured her heart.
The prince came home to Troezen: Phaedra was Queen of
    Athens.
There on the Acropolis, on the very Rock of Pallas,
She built a temple of Love looking seaward towards Troezen,
Where her heart wandered with her beloved far away; –
Still from that time this temple bears Hippolytus' name.
But Theseus, his hands stained with the blood of the Pallan-
    tides,
To purge his guilt, consented to live one year in exile,
And sailed with Phaedra his wife from Athens here to
    Troezen.
She now, poor wretch, groaning and maddened with the
    stabs of love,
Is dying, and in silence. No one in the palace knows
Her sickness. But not in secret shall her lust's full course be
    run.
I will reveal the truth to Theseus; all shall be shown.
This youth, who makes war with me, his own father Theseus
Shall kill with curses, by the power Poseidon King of the Sea

Gave him, that three requests of Theseus should not fail.
Phaedra shall save her honour, but must lose her life;
For I will not yield my rights through regard for her mis-
    fortunes,
But my enemies shall pay what they owe till I am satisfied.
Now I'll retire. Here comes Hippolytus, son of Theseus,
Home after his exertions in the hunting field, and with him
His whole pack of followers in full cry at his heels,
Singing hymns to Artemis! Little he knows that Death's
    gates
Are open now, and to-day's light is the last he shall see.

Exit.

Enter HIPPOLYTUS *with Huntsmen; also an Old Servant*

HIPPOLYTUS: Follow, and sing!
                Follow the bright Daughter of Heaven!
                Follow our guardian Maid,
                    Artemis!

HUNTSMEN: Child of Leto and of Zeus,
                Virgin Goddess Artemis,
                Great and holy, hear our song!
                    Greeting, joyful greeting,
                    Loveliest of maidens!
                You who haunt your kingly father's court,
                Tread at ease the broad sky's golden floor,
                    Loveliest of immortal maids,
                    Joyful greeting, Artemis!

HIPPOLYTUS: Goddess, for you I have twined this crown of
    flowers, gathered
Fresh from a virgin meadow, where no shepherd dares
To graze his flock, nor ever yet scythe swept,
But bees thread the Spring air over the maiden meadow.
There from the running stream Chastity waters the flowers;
And those whose untaught natures Holiness claims entire
May gather garlands there; and the impure may not.
Dear Mistress, take this flowery band for your bright hair,

Offered with reverent heart. I alone among mortals
Enjoy this honour; I am your companion, speak with you,
Hear your voice; only your face I do not see.
And may the end of my life's course be as the beginning!

SERVANT: My lord! – or, Prince! for only gods must be
called lord, – would you accept a word of good advice from
me?

HIPPOLYTUS: Of course! I should plainly be a fool if I would
not.

SERVANT: Then – you know an old law that is laid down for
men –

HIPPOLYTUS: No! What do you mean? Why are you asking
me this?

SERVANT: The law that says: Abhor pride and all unfriendli-
ness.

HIPPOLYTUS: Yes; a good law: haughtiness is always a hateful
thing.

SERVANT: And surely there is a charm in being open and
unreserved?

HIPPOLYTUS: Great charm; great profit too, and with little
trouble.

SERVANT: Do you not think this is as true for gods as for
men?

HIPPOLYTUS: Why, yes; if our mortal ways are like theirs.

SERVANT: Then why have you no prayer for – a great goddess?

HIPPOLYTUS: Be careful! A word may do harm. What goddess do you mean?

SERVANT: She stands here at your own door – Aphrodite!

HIPPOLYTUS: I greet her from far off: I am untainted.

SERVANT: Yet she is great; and her power is known and
feared.

HIPPOLYTUS: I have no love for gods worshipped by night.

SERVANT: My son, we must not neglect the honour due to
the gods.

HIPPOLYTUS: Gods may choose whom they will honour: so may mortals.

SERVANT: May the gods grant you wisdom, and good fortune too!

HIPPOLYTUS: Come, men, we'll go in; it is time for food. A loaded table's a cheerful sight after hunting. Rub down the horses: when I've had a good meal I'll take them out with the chariot and exercise them hard. – Your Aphrodite? No! To me she is nothing at all!

Exit HIPPOLYTUS *with Huntsmen.*

SERVANT: The ways of young men are not for us to copy. Queen Aphrodite! with humble hearts, as befits your servants, we worship you. You must forgive young blood, and the bold spirit that blurts foolish words against you. Forget that you heard him speak! You are a god: and the wisdom of gods must be wiser than men.

Exit.

Enter CHORUS *of Troezenian Women.*

CHORUS: You have heard of the rocky fountain   [*Strophe* 1
Where water gushes streaming from the heart of the earth,
Where they dip pails in the pool:
A friend of mine was there,
Rinsing rich-coloured clothes in the rill-water
And laying them to dry on the sun-baked rock:
She was the first to tell me about the Queen;

How she pines on a sick bed,   [*Antistrophe* 1
Keeps always within doors,
Clouding her golden head in the fine folds of her veil.
This is the third day, they say,
That her lovely lips refuse the gift of the Earth-Mother,
The innocent body of bread.
What storm is wrecking her life she will not tell;
But she longs to moor in the sad harbour of death.

Hers is no wild ecstasy   [*Strophe* 2
  Sent by Hecate or Pan,
Mountain-frenzy, Corybantic wandering
  By Cybele's power possessed.
      Has she sinned, neglecting
      Immemorial offerings,
Oil and honey for the Huntress Artemis?
  Wrath of gods can range and reach
      Every shore and island
      Through the salt sea's eddies.

  Or is Theseus' heart beguiled?   [*Antistrophe* 2
  Is your kingly husband false,
Following pleasure in some slave-girl's secret bed?
  Has some traveller from Crete
  Sailed with news of sorrow
  To our friendly harbour?
Are your kindred torn with trouble far away,
  That such bitter anguish
  Makes your bed your prison?

But women are always weak, and their
    ways are strange;   [*Epode*
Their very being is a blend of terror and helplessness
At the pains and follies their sex inherits.
I have felt this fear thrill through my own womb;
But I cried to the heavenly helper of all women,
    Artemis of the arrows;
And always – the gods be praised! – she came to my deep
    need.

Look! The old Nurse is coming to the door,
Bringing Queen Phaedra into the fresh air.
Her sad face is more clouded than before.
The Queen! How weak she is, how pale!
I long to know what has so wasted her.

Enter, from the palace, PHAEDRA *supported by the* NURSE.
Attendants bring a couch for her.

NURSE: Oh, the sickness and pain of this cruel world!
What can I do for you? How can I tell?
Here you are, in the light, under the clear sky;
We have brought your bed from the palace.
It was here that you begged and longed to come;
Soon you will change your mind and fret for your room
again.
Each minute cheats you, nothing gives you pleasure;
You hate what you have, and crave for what you have not.
Better to be sick, which is a single trouble,
Than wait on the sick, which troubles both heart and hand.
Man's life from birth to death is sorrow and pain,
With never pause or relief;
And when we are dead, is there a happier world?
Knowledge is hidden from us in clouds and darkness.
Since we can know no other kind of life,
Since the world of the dead is a mystery,
It seems we must blindly love, for what it is worth,
Our little gleam of light,
And follow our foolish course content with tales.

PHAEDRA: Support me, my friends, and lift my head;
The strength of my limbs has melted away.
Hold my white hands, my shapely arms!
This braided veil is a weight on my head, –
Off with it! Now let my hair fall round my shoulders.

NURSE: Patience, my child! Lie still, you will tire yourself!
If you are quiet and keep a brave heart
Your illness will be easier to bear.
We are mortal, and so must suffer.

PHAEDRA: If I could kneel by a well-side in the fresh dew
And drink a cupful of clear water!
If I could lie under the poplar-trees
And rest deep in the waving grass!

E   B

NURSE: Speak low, child! You must not scatter your words
      So loud and recklessly! There are people here!
      Your speech careers wildly on wheels of madness.

PHAEDRA: Come, take me! I am going
      Out to the hills and the woods, the pine-forests
      Where hounds pace after blood
      And press close on the spotted deer!
      O gods! were I there, shouting to the pack,
      Lifting the lance to my hair bright in the wind,
      Hurling the barbed blade!

NURSE: What is it, child, you are fretting for?
      What are hounds and the hunt to you?
      Why so in love with water from a spring?
      If you are thirsty,
      Here by the palace-wall a stream runs down the hill!

PHAEDRA: Lady of the Salt Mere,
      Artemis, lover of bold horsemanship!
      O for your level rides,
      And the tamed strength of a Thessaly horse under my hand!

NURSE: What next will you say? This is madness, child!
      You were craving first
      To hunt wild beasts in a mountain glade;
      Now, for a horse on the dry sandy track.
      Here's a task for a prophet indeed, to guess
      What god drives you beside yourself
      And strikes your senses from you!

PHAEDRA: What have I done? I have been wandering.
      My mind went from me – where? where? I was mad,
      A god touched me with madness. Oh, my grief!
      Dear Nurse, my veil again; I am ashamed
      To think what I have said. Cover my face.
      My tears fall down, and I am hot with shame.
      To come back to a right mind is agony,
      And no less agony to remain mad.
      It is best, then, to feel nothing, and so die!

NURSE [*veiling her*]: There, child, there! How soon
Shall my face too be veiled with death?
I have lived long, and learnt much.
Since we must die, it would be better,
In making friends, never to go too far,
Or open the depths of our heart to anyone.
The ties of love ought to lie loosely on us,
Easy to break or bind.
For one heart to endure the pain of two,
As I suffer for her, is a cruel burden.
They say that steadfast devotion
Brings with it more trouble than pleasure,
And is an enemy to life and health.
So I think that in this as in other things
It is best not to go too far;
And any wise man will say the same.

CHORUS: Madam, we see the Queen's distress and are sorry
for her; but what her illness is we cannot understand. We
would like to ask you, her old and trusted servant: will you
not tell us?

NURSE: I know nothing. I have questioned her, but she will
not speak.

CHORUS: Do you not know how, or when, this trouble first
began?

NURSE: The answer is still the same: to all such questions she
is silent.

CHORUS: How frail and wasted she looks!

NURSE: No wonder: she has eaten nothing for three days.

CHORUS: Is she out of her mind? Or does she mean to die?

NURSE: She means to die. She is starving herself to death.

CHORUS: Strange that her husband should accept it calmly!

NURSE: She hides her illness from him, tells him she is
well.

CHORUS: Does he not look at her face and see for himself?

NURSE: Just now it happens he is away from Troezen.

CHORUS: Can you not compel her to speak? Anything, to discover the cause of this sickness and these delusions!

NURSE: I have tried everything and achieved nothing; but I want to do my best, and I will not give up even now. And you, friends, are here to witness that I am one to stand by my lady in time of trouble. [*She turns to* PHAEDRA.]

Dear child, let us both forget the things we said before. Smooth away this terrible look from your brow: be my dear daughter! Don't wander any more – I was wrong to follow you, prying into your thoughts; I will be wiser. Is your sickness something you cannot speak of openly? There are women here to help with remedies. But if your trouble can be told to a man, only speak, and we will consult doctors. Well: not a word? My dear, if I have spoken foolishly, correct me; if well, say you agree. Do not sit there dumb! Speak! One word! Look at me! It is no use. [*She weeps.*] All our trouble leads to nothing, and we are as far off as ever; she would not soften before, and still refuses. Listen to me, my lady: be if you will more stubborn than the sea, – but what of your sons, if you should die? Who will take their part? They will never inherit their father's palace – no, by Hippolyta, Queen of the riding Amazons! She has a son whom your boys will serve as slaves, a bastard nursing the ambition of his royal birth, one you know well: Hippolytus!

PHAEDRA: No! No!

NURSE: Ha! Does that touch you?

PHAEDRA: You kill me! Nurse, by all the gods I implore you never again to speak of him!

NURSE: There! You are not out of your mind, far from it! And yet you still refuse both to save your own life and to help your children.

PHAEDRA: I love my children; but something else is drowning me in despair.

NURSE: My daughter, – your hands are free from blood?

PHAEDRA: My hands are pure; but my heart is defiled.

NURSE: Defiled? What? With some wrong done to you by an enemy?

PHAEDRA: No, no enemy! It is no more his will than mine that he should destroy me.

NURSE: Theseus! Has he done you some injury?

PHAEDRA: No! May I prove as guiltless towards him!

NURSE: What then is this terror that is dragging you to your grave?

PHAEDRA: Leave me to my sin. I do not sin against *you*.

NURSE: I will not leave you if I can help it. If I fail it will be your fault.

PHAEDRA: Will you try to force me? Let my hand go!

NURSE: I will not! I will cling to you until you tell me!

PHAEDRA: Poor soul! The truth would be terrible to you too.

NURSE: What could be worse to me than to see you suffer?

PHAEDRA: To tell would kill you; but what I am doing is for my honour –

NURSE: If so, to speak of it will add to your honour before the world.

PHAEDRA: – I am finding a way to bring honour out of shame.

NURSE: Then I am right in begging you to tell me – how can you hide it?

PHAEDRA: For the gods' sake leave me and let go my hand!

NURSE: Never, while you refuse what you owe to me!

PHAEDRA: It is true! I owe it. I will tell you what you ask.

NURSE: I will be quiet. Now it is for you to speak.

PHAEDRA: O my mother! What dreadful, pitiful lust raged within you!

NURSE: You mean her lust for the bull? Or what do you mean, my child?

PHAEDRA: And you too, O my sister, whom Dionysus desired – how love made you suffer!

NURSE: Why speak of them? Those tales are best forgotten.

PHAEDRA: The curse that destroyed them I now inherit.

NURSE: You frighten me! What are you going to say now?

PHAEDRA: My misery began with them. It is no new thing.

NURSE: You tell me no more of what I long to hear.

PHAEDRA: The words that you want me to say – if only you could speak them for me!

NURSE: I am no magician to read hidden thoughts.

PHAEDRA: When they say that one is in love, what do they mean by love?

NURSE: Oh, my child! It is the sweetest of all things, – yet full of pain.

PHAEDRA: It seems I have found the pain, but no sweetness.

NURSE: What are you saying? You love a man? What man?

PHAEDRA: Why, who should it be? It is he! The Amazon's son!

NURSE: Hippolytus!

PHAEDRA: You spoke his name, not I.

NURSE: Oh, my child! What are you saying? Oh! you have broken my heart! Oh, friends, how can I bear it? How can I go on living? Oh! this hateful life, this accursed day! [*She collapses to the ground, and the* CHORUS *come to help her.*] No! Let me fall, leave me alone; I want to die and be at peace! I am dying, my life is over! . . . What does it mean? Here is a pure-hearted woman, with no desire to do wrong, yet lusting after wickedness against her will! [*Defiantly.*] Aphrodite is no goddess! No! She has brought this disaster on Phaedra and on me and on the royal house, – she is something more than a goddess – something greater!

CHORUS: Did you hear? Oh, did you hear
    The Queen's pitiful cry,
    Born of a crueller blow
    Than human heart can bear?
    Beloved Queen, let me die
    Before my heart should know
    Your heart's despair!
    Oh, Phaedra, daughter of sorrow!

Oh, sorrow, nurse of our race!
Deadly calamity, dragged into sudden light!
How can you live to face,
Hour by hour, the horror that hangs its threat
Over your house, unknown as yet?
The Queen of Love sent you a strange star,
Princess of Crete!
We see now where it will sink and set.

PHAEDRA: Women of Troezen, who live here on the outer
threshold of Peloponnese: I have at times lain long awake in
the night, thinking how other lives than mine have been
shattered; and I believe that such misfortune does not arise
from inborn folly, since often those who suffer are wise and
good. But this is how we should regard the matter: we know
and see what is right, yet fail to carry it out. Some fail
through sloth, others through valuing some pleasure more
than goodness; and life offers us many pleasures.

Listen: I will tell you the path my thoughts followed. When
love struck me, I searched for the best way to endure the
wound. My first resolve was to let slip no word, to hide what
I suffered; for there is no trusting the tongue, which knows
how to instruct others in wisdom, but invites disaster by its
own folly. Next, I prepared to endure this madness as I
ought, by overcoming it with self-control. Finally, when I
still did not succeed in mastering this love, I determined
that the best plan for me, beyond all contradiction, was to
die. That is the decision I have taken; that is why I did not
choose to thwart my own purpose with any kind of healing
drug. If I do what is right, I would not wish to hide it, any
more than to display my sins before witnesses. I knew that
both the thing I craved, and the craving itself, was a sin. I knew
also, too well, that I was a woman: a mark for the world's
contempt. Whatever woman first was false to her husband
with other men, misery and death destroy her! It was from
noble houses that this plague first spread among women:

when the great choose dishonour, the common herd will do the same. I hate women whose tongues talk of chastity, who in secret are bold in every sin! Queen Aphrodite, born from the sea's purity! how can they look into their husbands' eyes, and not shudder lest sheltering darkness and guilty walls should speak? . . .

Friends, it is for this I am dying, that I may never be found guilty of disgracing my husband and my children. I want my sons to go back to the city of cities, to Athens, and hold their heads high and speak like free men there, and not blush for their mother. To live burdened with the secret of a parent's sin will enslave the boldest spirit. Only an upright heart and a clear conscience, they say, gives a man strength to wrestle with life; while those whose hearts are evil, sooner or later – as a young girl sees the truth in her glass – so they, when Time holds up his mirror, find their own sin revealed. May I never be found among them!

CHORUS: It is true: virtue, wherever it appears, is a beautiful thing; and the fruit of virtue in this life is a good name.

NURSE: My lady, when I heard what had happened to you, at the first shock I was terrified: now I begin to reflect how foolish I was. In human life second thoughts often prove to be wiser. What has happened to you is nothing extraordinary or hard to understand. The fever of Aphrodite has fastened on you: you are in love. What is strange in that? Why, so are countless others! And do you therefore mean to lose your life for love? Then surely there is a hard road ahead for all lovers now and to come, if their duty is to die! When Love sweeps on in the fulness of her power, there is no resisting. She steals gently on those who yield to her; but those she finds arrogant and haughty she takes and – what do you suppose? – tramples in the dust! Love rides on clouds and strides through the swollen sea. The whole world was born from Love; she sows every seed; every living creature on earth sprang from that sweet desire which is

her gift to us. Those who possess pictures drawn in times
past, or who spend their days pursuing the arts, – they know
that Zeus once lusted for Semele, they know that once the
lovely goddess of the glowing dawn stole away Cephalus and
took him to live among the gods, because she loved him.
Yet Cephalus and she live in the sky, and show no haste to
quit the company of gods. Events have proved too strong for
them; and they, believe me, are content. And you: do you
refuse to submit? Your father, it seems, should have be-
gotten you upon terms, or looked for other gods, if you're
resolved to find fault with the laws of Nature. I ask you:
how many good and sensible husbands see their wives un-
faithful and look the other way? How many fathers help
their love-sick sons to get what they want? Why, the true
wisdom for mortals is to keep faults well hidden. A builder
doesn't plane and polish the rafters in the roof! and it's not
for us mortals to struggle after a tiresome perfection. In any
case, how do you think you're going to swim clear of this
flood of trouble you've met with? You are mortal, child:
if the good you find in life outweighs the ill, you will be
extremely fortunate. My dear daughter, soften your stubborn heart; do not blaspheme! What is it but blasphemy, to
wish yourself stronger than a god? You are in love: then
bear – and dare – what the god has willed. You are stricken:
turn the stroke to your own good. Why, there are spells and
soothing charms; we'll find a medicine for you. Trouble
may wait a long time for men to mend it, if we women take
no hand in the matter.

CHORUS: Her advice is more practical, Phaedra, for your
present need; yet you, I feel, are right. Though it may be my
approval is harder for you to accept, and more painful to
hear, than her reproaches.

PHAEDRA: This is what brings ruin on fine cities and ancient
houses – fair speech, too fair by far! Instead of saying what
you think will please me, show me a way to save my honour.

NURSE: This is mere high-flown talk. Fine sentiments will not
help you: you must have your man! He must be told in plain
words what has happened, and won over without delay. If
this were not a matter of life and death, if you were still a
chaste-minded woman, I would never encourage you so far
for your own lust and pleasure; but now we must fight for
your life, – and there is nothing wrong in this.

PHAEDRA: Nothing wrong! It is horrible! Be silent, never
speak such shameful words again!

NURSE: Shameful, – maybe; but more use to you than good
words. Better do what I say, and live, than die for a vain
boast of chastity.

PHAEDRA: No, for the gods' sake! What you say is plausible,
but vile. Go no further! I have disciplined my heart to
endure this. If you are so eloquent for evil, I shall fall now
into the very pit I shrink from.

NURSE: If you feel so, – you should not have sinned at heart.
Well, you did: now obey me – and be as ungrateful as you
like. I have indoors a drug for the soothing of love – I have
only now thought of it; it will bring you into no disgrace,
no distress of mind, but it will cure you of your passion, if
only you are not faint-hearted.

PHAEDRA: This drug – is it an ointment, or a draught?

NURSE: I don't know. Look for help, my girl, not explanations.

PHAEDRA: You may be too clever, and ruin me. I dread it.

NURSE: Then you would dread anything. What is it you are
afraid of?

PHAEDRA: Of your saying any word about me to Hippolytus.

NURSE: Leave that to me, child. I know what to do. [Aside]
Great Queen Aphrodite, only stand by me now, and help!
For what else I have in mind, a word to our friend in the
palace will be enough.

                    Exit NURSE. PHAEDRA remains.

CHORUS:

   O Love, immortal Power,   *[Strophe* 1
Love, dropping desire like dew on yearning eyes,
   Love, whose triumphant arms
Ravish the conquered soul with sweetest ecstasy!
   Come not in cruelty,
Never with ruthless violence invade my life!
   Fiery stroke of star or sun
Is less to fear than Aphrodite's dart
Which flies from the hand of Love, the child of Zeus,
   To madden a mortal heart.

   In vain by Alpheus' banks,   *[Antistrophe* 1
In vain at the Pythian shrine shall sacrifice multiply,
   And the blood of bulls pour forth,
Toll from the pastures of Greece to Apollo and Artemis;
   While Eros, Master of man,
   Who holds Aphrodite's key
   To her chamber of sweet delight, –
   Him in our prayers we slight:
Love, whose coming has brought, since the world began,
   Death and calamity!

Iole, Princess of Oechalia,   *[Strophe* 2
Was once a free and taintless virgin,
A maiden unmatched with man;
But Aphrodite tore her from her home,
A wild nymph, helpless and frantic;
And there, amidst blood and smoke,
With dying groans for her bridal-hymn,
Gave her to the son of Alcmene
To carry weeping across the sea.

O holy wall of Thebes,   *[Antistrophe* 2
O lips of the Dircean spring,

You with one voice could tell
How terrible is the advent of Aphrodite!
When upon Semele thunder and flame descended,
And her womb gave birth to Bacchus, the child of Zeus,
Aphrodite laid her to sleep,
A bride in the bed of Death.
For the breath of her terror is felt in every land,
And swift as a bee's flight
Is the path of her power.

PHAEDRA: Women, be quiet! ... Oh, the last blow has fallen!

CHORUS: We will be quiet. But this sounds ominous!

PHAEDRA: Wait! I want to hear exactly what they are saying.

CHORUS: Something terrible is happening in the palace. Phaedra, what is it?

PHAEDRA: Oh! Why must I suffer so? It is unbearable!

CHORUS: What is unbearable?
              What is this anguished cry?
              Tell us, what fearful word
              Fell on your ears like Fate?

PHAEDRA: It is — my death! Come, stand near the door and listen. Do you hear what an uproar is rising there?

CHORUS: You are beside the door:
              For you the house utters a voice! Tell me, then,
              What horror you heard,
              Tell me, what has been done?

PHAEDRA: It is the son of the riding Amazon, Hippolytus, cursing and abusing my old servant.

CHORUS: Yes, I can hear the sound,
              Yet not a word is clear!
              How can I tell? Oh, it was clear to you,
              The cry that came from the house!

PHAEDRA: Ah, listen! Yes, too clear! He calls her 'filthy bawd', damns her for treason to her master's bed!

CHORUS:

> No, no! What shall we do?
>
> Lady, you are betrayed!
>
> What plan can I offer?
>
> Your secret shown to the world,
>
> Your life and hope laid in the dust by the hand of a friend!

PHAEDRA: She has told him the fatal truth about me. She did it for love, to cure my suffering; but it was wrong!

CHORUS: What now? What way out is there? What will you do?

PHAEDRA: I do not know, — only this: that to die at once is the sole escape from this torture.

Enter HIPPOLYTUS, *followed by the* NURSE

HIPPOLYTUS: O Mother Earth! O unfolding radiance of the sun! What things I have heard! What words unspeakable have been spoken!

NURSE: Be quiet, lad, or someone will hear this clamour!

HIPPOLYTUS: How can I be quiet after what I have listened to?

NURSE: I beg you, I kiss your hand — dear boy, be quiet!

HIPPOLYTUS: Keep your hands off my clothes! You shall not touch me.

NURSE: For the gods' sake, have pity! Don't tell what I said to you! It would kill me.

HIPPOLYTUS: Kill you? Your words were harmless, you said!

NURSE: What I said, my son, was not for everyone to hear.

HIPPOLYTUS: Honest words should not be hushed up: let everyone hear!

NURSE: My boy, do not slight the oath you swore me!

HIPPOLYTUS: My tongue swore: the oath does not bind my heart.

NURSE: What will you do, child? Destroy your friend?

HIPPOLYTUS: Friend? God forbid I should have any such friend!

NURSE: Forgive! We are human; we cannot help doing wrong.

HIPPOLYTUS: O Zeus! Why have you plagued this world with so vile and worthless a thing as woman? If it was your pleasure to plant a mortal stock, why must women be the renewers of the race? Better that men should come to your temples and put down a price, each what he could afford, – buy themselves children in embryo for gold or silver and get their money's worth; then they could live at home like free men, without women! Why, for proof that woman is an evil pest, – her father, after begetting and bringing her up, pays out a dowry to find her a home, and so gets rid of her; while whoever welcomes the viper to his bosom gleefully decks her out with gauds and gowns like a sacred statue, heaping beauty upon hatefulness, poor wretch, and squanders his inheritance. What choice has he? If he marries noble blood, he beds with his shrew and makes the best of it; or if he finds a good wife in a worthless family, with that much comfort he counters his ill-luck. For an easy life, marry a nobody, and keep her worthless and witless on a pedestal. I hate a woman who is clever – a woman who thinks more than becomes a woman; I would not have her in my house! For passion engenders wickedness the more readily in clever women; while the simple are kept from wantonness by lack of wit. A wife should have no servant ever come near her, she should live attended by dumb savage beasts, who could neither understand her nor speak to her. As it is, unchaste wives sit at home scheming lechery, while their servants traffic their schemes out to the world: – you for one, coming like a she-devil to invite me to incest with my father's wife! I'll flush your filthy words from my ears with floods of water! Do you think I could so sin, when I feel polluted merely by hearing you?

Listen: I let you trap me into swearing silence. I fear the gods, and that saves you; otherwise I would at once have told my father the whole story. Instead, I shall now leave the palace until he comes back; and I shall say nothing; but I shall come back with my father, and then I shall observe how you and your mistress meet his eye. You at least will brazen it out – I know what you're made of. – Curse the whole race of you! I can never hate you enough. Ha! They tell me I always say the same thing: well, women, it seems, always *are* the same thing. So whoever can teach women to be chaste may forbid me to tread their name in the dust!

Exit.

CHORUS: How cruel a curse it is to be born a woman!
           Who would not pity us?
           What shift, what turn, what plea,
           After the first faltering,
           Can loose us from the clamp of guilt?

PHAEDRA: I have met what I deserved.
           Earth and sunlight, show me where to fly
           Out of the clutch of Fate!
           Where can I hide my anguish?
           What god or man can give to my guilty soul
           Safety or help or counsel?
           I am caught in toils of torment;
           There is no escape for the living:
           I sink under the scourge of Chance.

CHORUS: Lady, I weep with you. The harm is done; your servant's plans have failed disastrously.

PHAEDRA [*to* NURSE]: You vile, treacherous murderess, see what you have done to me! May Zeus who gave me life blast you with fire and grind you to dust! Did I not try to prevent what you were plotting? Did I not forbid you to speak a word of what now drags me in the dirt? You spoke: and your treason robs even my death of honour. Now – some new plan. Hippolytus, white-hot with rage, will carry your foul words to his father and denounce me; go complaining to old Pittheus, fill the whole land with his outrageous tale!

Curse you! Curse all officious fools who thrust their wicked help on their friends to ruin them!

NURSE: My lady, I have done you wrong; you may well blame me. The wound pricks, and overcomes your judgement. Yet, if you'll listen to me, I can speak for myself. I nursed you; I am your friend; I tried to find a remedy for your trouble; and I was unlucky. With better luck, I would have been called a wise woman. After all, wisdom is only happening to guess right.

PHAEDRA: So! This is your just amends to me – to follow up your treachery with argument!

NURSE: We are wasting time in talk. I admit I was un-wise; but, my daughter, there's hope, there's life, even now!

PHAEDRA: Stop! Not another word! You gave me advice before, and help too; and both were wicked. Get out of my sight! Scheme for your own affairs, and I will set mine in order!

Exit NURSE.

Noblewomen of Troezen, I ask you to do me this favour: bury deep in silence all that you have heard here to-day.

CHORUS: By holy Artemis, daughter of Zeus, I swear to dis-close nothing of what has happened to you.

PHAEDRA: That is well. Listen, my friends – I have said this before –: I have a remedy for my present plight; one that will ensure an honourable future for my sons, and help me in face of to-day's calamity. The royal house of Crete shall forfeit no reputation through me. After this shame, to face Theseus would be too high a price for one life.

CHORUS: What are you going to do, that is so dreadful and so final?

PHAEDRA: To die. By what means, I will decide for myself.

CHORUS: In God's name, no!

PHAEDRA: You too must school me; I know my part. To-day

I'll be rid of life, and give joy to my immortal murderess.
Love is without mercy: I shall die defeated. Yet my death
shall be a curse on another's life, and teach him not to
trample on my agony. He shall have an equal share in my
suffering, and learn to be gentle!

Exit PHAEDRA.

CHORUS:

    O to escape and hide   [*Strophe* 1
High among steep and secret rocks!
    At the touch of a god to change,
    To rise as a bird and ride
On feathered wings among soaring flocks!
    To wander far and free
Where the lost waters of Eridanus flow deep
    Down to an unknown sea;
Where for dead Phaethon the Sun's daughters weep,
      Dropping piteous tears that gleam
      Like amber in the purple stream!

And O for that quiet garden by the Western sea [*Antistrophe* 1
    Where the daughters of Evening sing
    Under the golden apple-tree;
    Where the bold sailor wandering
    Finds the Ocean-god has barred
His Westward path over the purple waste!
    Where huge Atlas lives to guard
    The solemn frontiers of the sky;
Where in Zeus' palace fountains of ambrosial wine
    Flow by the festal couch divine,
    While holy Earth heaps high
    Her fruits of rarest taste
To bless the immortal feast with bountiful supply!

    White-winged Cretan ship,   [*Strophe* 2
That brought my lady Phaedra from her wealthy home

Over the salt swell of the pounding sea, –
    White sails for the joy of a bride,
    To veil the black fate waiting!
    Heavy with omen was her course
From Crete to Athens, queen of mainland cities,
When at Peiraeus her seamen leapt ashore
And looped their plaited hawsers on the quay;
    Dark again was the hour
When from the rocky harbour of Munychion
The royal progress parted for Troezen.

Thence on Phaedra fell the fatal curse,   [*Antistrophe* 2
When Aphrodite with a cruel unholy lust
    Shattered her helpless heart!
    Now the storm of her distress
    Drives her, a sinking wreck,
    Alone to her marriage-chamber.
    From the high beam she will tie
    Close round her white neck the noose:
    This her one choice, to die!
Thus with reverence learnt for her immortal enemy,
And prizing a fair name above her life,
She will win release of heart from her tormenting love.

A voice is heard shouting from the palace.

VOICE: Oh, help, help! Anyone who is in the house, come
and help! She is hanging – the Queen, the wife of Theseus!

CHORUS: Oh! She has kept her word! Oh, Phaedra,
Phaedra! She is dead, dead! the Queen! Hung high in a
strangling rope!

VOICE: Come quickly! Bring a knife, a sword, anything to
cut this cord from her neck!

CHORUS: A. Friends, what shall we do? Ought we to go
inside and untie the noose and free her?

    B. Why, where are the young men who attend her? It is
never safe to interfere.

VOICE: Poor lady, she is dead! Lay her limbs out straight. Oh, what a tale to have to tell my master!

CHORUS: Did you hear? Poor Phaedra, she is dead; they are already laying out her body.

Enter THESEUS, *attended by the royal guard. His head is crowned with the garland worn by those who have received a favourable answer from an oracle.*

THESEUS: Tell me, women, – what was that outcry in the palace? What I heard was the voices of servants weeping. [*There is silence.*] This is strange: I return home from a solemn mission of piety – and my home receives me with shut doors, not a word of welcome or greeting! ... I hope nothing has happened to Pittheus? He is well advanced in years; yet his departure from this house would be a grief to me.

CHORUS: What has happened, Theseus, has not touched the old. It is the young whose death will break your heart.

THESEUS: What? Is one of my children's lives stolen from me?

CHORUS: No, it is still more terrible: their mother is dead.

THESEUS: What do you say? My wife dead? What happened?

CHORUS: She made a noose with a rope and hanged herself.

THESEUS: But why? Was it some numbing stroke of grief? What could cause so dreadful an act?

CHORUS: That is all I know, Theseus. I have just now come to the palace to mourn for your loss.

THESEUS: Phaedra – dead! ... Why have I crowned my head with this garland of leaves? *Here* is my answer from the oracle! – Ho, there! Servants! Unbar the doors and open! Open them wide, let me see my dead wife, whose death is death to me!

The doors open, showing PHAEDRA *dead.*

CHORUS:
Weep for the Queen, tears for her tears!
Phaedra, your agony and your act alike
Must banish peace from this house!

How could you dare a death so hideous, so unholy,
A prey to your own pitiless hand?
Poor soul, what power dims your brightness in death?

THESEUS:

O the torture of life! In this city of exile
I have seen surely the utmost of the grief appointed for me!
O Fate, like a cruel heel crushing me and my house,
A nameless foul infection from some pursuing fiend,
Corrupting, annihilating life and the love of life!
I strain despairing eyes over my sea of misery,
And my hope of safety vanishes, for the shore is out of sight
And life is a mounting wave I have not strength to surmount.
    What reason, Phaedra, what malicious chance,
    What fated cruelty can I accuse?
    As a bird from my hand you have vanished,
Swooped swift and daring into the pit of darkness
And left me tears for your death and anguish for your
        despair!
    Far from here this harvest grew;
    Long ago a sin was sown;
        Fruit the gods have ripened
        For my grief I gather.

CHORUS: King, this sorrow falls not on your soul alone:
            Many share it, weeping
            A dear wife departed.

THESEUS:

To go into the dark! Now let me die, and pass
To the world under the earth, into the joyless dark!
Since you, dearer than all, are at my side no longer,
And the death you have dealt is more than the death that has
    swallowed you.
Who will tell me the truth? Whence, my wife, could it
    come, –
This chance, whose murderous blow fell on your tortured
    heart?

What happened? Shall I be told? Or does my palace harbour
A horde of lying lackeys? Phaedra! my heart is broken!
Friends, pity me, who have lived to see such pain
Ravage my home! No words can speak of it,
No human heart bear it. My life is over.

Now my house is desolate,
And my children motherless.
You, the dearest, best, of all
That the dazzling sun surveys
Or the star-eyed evening, –
You are gone for ever!

As THESEUS *has been speaking, the* CHORUS *have noticed a
letter tied to* PHAEDRA'S *wrist.*

CHORUS:
Theseus, I pity you for the storm that wrecks your home.
Yet, while I have watched your sorrow with tear-filled eyes,
Still I tremble with deeper dread for the terror to come!

THESEUS: Look! Look here! A letter fastened to her dear
hand! What does this mean? Will it tell me something new?
Surely, she has written her dying wishes, begging me to
remember our marriage and our children. Rest easy,
Phaedra! My house and bed shall never be entered by
another woman! See, the impression of her golden signet
brings me her greeting from the dead! Now to untwist the
cord from the seal, and see what this letter has to tell me.

CHORUS: Here is a crueller pain, a deeper horror
Sent by the gods to crown the rest! If it were I, –
Knowing the truth, how could I bear my life?
The royal house heaped in ruin, never to rise!
Gods have pity! Strike not down!
Hear and help us! ... In his eyes,
See, so grimly staring,
Portents of disaster!

THESEUS: Oh, oh! Horror upon horror, blow upon blow!
Beyond endurance, beyond speech! Oh!

They know

CHORUS: What now? If it is for us to hear, tell us!

THESEUS:

The letter! It shrieks, it howls, horrors indelible!

I am crushed; where can I escape? What I have seen has killed me.

A voice from the letter speaks, and tells – what things! what things!

CHORUS: What are you saying, Theseus? Something dreadful must follow.

THESEUS:

A thing so dreadful that I scarcely can force my tongue
To utter it. Yet I will speak now. Listen, O city!

Hippolytus has braved the holy eye of Zeus and done violence to my wife's honour!

Yes, Poseidon my father, you promised me three curses: with one of them strike down my son! If they were good curses you gave me, let him not live out this day!

Praying

CHORUS: My lord, in heaven's name, take your prayer back! You are wrong – you will know it later; only trust me!

THESEUS: There is no taking back. I will not only curse but banish him from the land. If the one fails he shall feel the other. Either Poseidon will honour my curse and send his corpse below, or else as a stranger wandering the earth, an outcast from his country, he shall drain his despicable life to the dregs.

CHORUS: Why, look! Here, this very moment, comes your son himself, Hippolytus! King Theseus, calm this dangerous anger, and consider what will be best for yourself and your family.

Enter HIPPOLYTUS, *with Huntsmen.*

HIPPOLYTUS: Father, I heard your outcry and came at once. What trouble has caused your distress I do not know; but I wish you would tell me. ... Oh! What do I see? It is your wife, Father – dead! Dead? How is it possible? I had only just left her; a short time ago she was alive! What has hap-

pened to her? How did she die? ... Father, I am asking you
to tell me! Will you not speak? This is no time to be silent!
I know that to insist out of season on being told everything
is called idle curiosity; but I am a friend – something more
than a friend. Surely, Father, you should not hide trouble
from me!

THESEUS: Oh, the futile folly of men! Why do they teach arts
innumerable, contrive and search out every other thing, –
when one knowledge they cannot win, one quarry they
have not caught: the skill to teach wisdom to the brutish.

HIPPOLYTUS: He would certainly be a clever instructor who
could drive sense into a fool. But, Father, this is not the
time for philosophical discourse. Sorrow, I fear, is making
you talk wildly.

THESEUS: Oh, there should be somewhere a touchstone of
human hearts, which men could trust to tell them the truth
about their friends, who is loyal and who treacherous!
Every man should have two voices, the one truthful, the
other – natural; so that his lying voice might be refuted by
the true; and we should not be duped.

HIPPOLYTUS: What? Has one of your friends contrived to
slander me to you and make you suspect my innocence? I
am bewildered, astonished! Your words are crazed, you
have taken leave of your wits!

THESEUS: The heart of man! Is there any vileness it will turn
from? Will barefaced wickedness ever find its limit? If
crime is to bulk bigger with each new generation, new
depths of villainy be revealed age after age, the gods will
need to create a second earth to house liars and lechers.
Look at this man! my own son, who would pollute my
marriage-bed, – and is proved guilty by the damning witness
of her dead hand. Come, show your face – foul as you are,
look your father in the eyes! So you – you are the man above
men who keeps the company of gods! Yours is the chaste
life unsmirched with evil! Who believes your bragging?

Who charges gods with such ignorance and folly? Not I!
So, now flaunt your purity! Play the quack with your flesh-
less diets! Take Orpheus for your lord and prophet and
wallow in frenzied adoration of his wordy vapourings! Yes,
you are exposed! Of such men let the world take warning
and beware! They pursue their prey with lofty words and
low cunning. – Oh, she is dead: do you think that will save
you? No, vile criminal, it is the prime evidence of your
guilt. What oaths or arguments could outweigh her witness
and acquit you? You will say that she hated you; that there
will always be war between the bastard and the true-born.
Was she so poor a bargainer with her life, that she would
throw away all its sweetness to spite you? Or will you tell
me that young men are free from folly, women born to it?
Well I know that young men are no steadier than women,
when Aphrodite stirs the hot blood in them. Indeed, their
sex makes them even more headstrong.

  Ah! why should I fight down your defence, when her
dead body blazons its evidence to my eyes? Out of this land
to exile! Go, I say! Never come near the god-built walls of
Athens, cross no frontier that my sword guards! I tell you,
if I weaken before this outrage, the Isthmian bandit Sinis
shall deny that I killed him, and call me boaster; and the sea-
washed rocks where Sciron met his end shall forget the
weight of my hand against evildoers!

CHORUS: How can any mortal man be called happy? Until
  to-day, Hippolytus, you were first in good fortune: now
  everything is reversed.

HIPPOLYTUS: Father, your passionate anger is terrible; and
  though what you say at first appears just, you will find it does
  not bear closer scrutiny. Though I have no skill to address a
  crowd, among a few equals I can speak with more confidence. And this is natural; just as those who seem fools
  among wise men can be eloquent before crowds. So, now
  that my whole life is in danger, I must be bold and speak.

And I will begin with the first charge you levelled at me, which you thought would leave me shattered and speechless. Look at this sky, this earth: in the length and breadth of them there is no man – deny it as you will – more pure in heart than I! I have learnt, first, to reverence the gods; then, to choose friends who keep their hands innocent, whose honour forbids them either to render me or expect from me any discreditable service. I do not mock those I live among, Father; I am the same to my friends absent or present. One sin you now think me convicted of has never touched me: to this day my body is chaste; I have not known a woman. I know nothing of such matters, more than I have heard men tell, or seen in pictures; which I have little desire to look at, for my mind is virgin. Perhaps you refuse to believe that I am pure: then it is for you to show what temptation was too strong for me. Was your wife more beautiful than all other women? Or did I hope, by winning her love, to become your heir? Any such hope would have been less vain than mad! Did I covet your place as king? For a wise man a throne has no attraction; to find pleasure in power is to be corrupted by it – there are many examples. No; my ambition is a different one: let me be first in the Grecian Games, and in politics take second place, and be happy with honest friends. In this way I am able to live my own life – and to live free from danger, which is a greater blessing than a crown.

That is all I have to say, except one thing: if a witness to my innocence were here to speak, and if Phaedra were alive to listen to my defence, then the event would guide your search for the guilty. As things are, I swear to you by Zeus, Guardian of oaths, and by the Earth, that I never touched your wife, never could have wished even to think of it. I pray that I may die in nameless dishonour, cityless, homeless, exile and vagabond, – may neither sea nor land receive my dead flesh, if there is sin in me! Whether it was fear that made Phaedra take her life I do not know; further than this it is impossible for me to speak. She kept her chastity, without possessing the virtue of chastity; I possess it, and have practised it to my own ruin.

CHORUS: Surely what you have said will suffice to clear you! Your solemn oaths to the gods must be believed.

THESEUS: Is he not a spellmonger, a cheat, hoping to master my mind with his smooth temper, after putting his father to open shame?

HIPPOLYTUS: It is *your* smooth temper that I wonder at, Father. If you were my son, and I in your place, I would have killed you, not corrected you with exile, if you had dared to touch my wife.

THESEUS: Indeed! How justly! No, you shall not die like that. Many a criminal would be glad of a quick death. No: since you have passed sentence on yourself, you shall wander an outcast from your country, on alien soil you shall drain the bitter lees of life, and earn a criminal's reward.

HIPPOLYTUS: What? You will do that? You will not wait for the witness of time to condemn me, but drive me out to-day?

THESEUS: Yes! beyond the outer ocean and the ends of the earth, if I had the power, so abominable to me is the sight of you!

HIPPOLYTUS: You spurn my sworn oath, you seek no guidance of priests, but banish me unjudged?

THESEUS: Priests! with their omens from birds that fly about overhead! To me they are nothing at all! This letter here is no soothsayer's riddle, and it proves you guilty.

HIPPOLYTUS: Why do I not unlock my lips? You gods, whom my silence honours, it is you who destroy me! – No: I will not speak. Nothing I might say now could carry weight where it would help me. To tell the truth would be to break my oath and gain nothing.

THESEUS: Still your cursed piety! It chokes me! What are you waiting for? Out of my land, I say!

HIPPOLYTUS: Out of your land? Which way shall I turn? Who of my friends will receive me, exiled on such a charge?

THESEUS: Who? Any that has a warm welcome for the defiler of men's wives, the bosom-friend of all iniquity!

HIPPOLYTUS: Oh, it is time indeed for tears and a broken heart, when my father thinks and truly believes that I am guilty.

THESEUS: The time for you to weep and be wise was the time when you cast off shame to dishonour your father's wife!

HIPPOLYTUS: Oh, if these walls could but cry out and speak for me, and witness whether I am so vile a man!

THESEUS: You are careful to fly for help to dumb witnesses; but the fact needs no tongue to prove you guilty.

HIPPOLYTUS: I wish for very pity that I could stand apart and behold myself, to shed tears for my own suffering!

THESEUS: No doubt! You are far more practised in self-worship than in self-control and honourable conduct to your father.

HIPPOLYTUS: My unhappy mother! I was born in bitterness of sorrow. May no one that I love ever be called bastard!

THESEUS: Guards! take him away! Do you not hear? I have already pronounced him banished.

HIPPOLYTUS: It will be the worse for any of them that touches me. Since you're so minded, thrust me out yourself!

THESEUS: I will do so, unless you obey me. Your exile does not touch my tears.

Exit THESEUS.

HIPPOLYTUS: My fate, then, is fixed. It is sad and cruel, that I know the truth, yet know no way to speak it. [*He turns to the figure of* ARTEMIS.] Goddess, daughter of Leto, most dear companion, and comrade in the hunt, I shall live exiled for ever from glorious Athens! Farewell, my city;

farewell, land of Erechtheus; farewell, plain of Troezen, rich in the vigorous delights of youth! I take my last look now, speak my last word to you. And you too, lads that have grown up with me here, – come, say good-bye to me and see me to the border. Though even my own father denies it, you will never meet a man more honourable.

Exit HIPPOLYTUS *with his men.*

CHORUS:

When I remember that the gods take thought   [*Strophe* 1
For human life, often in hours of grief
  To me this faith has brought
  Comfort and heart's relief.

Yet, though deep in my hope perception lies
Wistful, experience grows and faith recedes:
  Men's fortunes fall and rise
  Not answering to their deeds.

Change follows change; Fate purposeless and blind
Uproots us from familiar soil:
  The longest life can find
  No rest from travel and toil.

This is my prayer: may divine providence fulfil [*Antistrophe* 1
  All my heart's will,
  And bless my days with wealth, and guard
My life from pain, and keep my soul unscarred.

The dauntless stern resolve is not for me,
Nor the fair face masking the false intent;
  Rather my choice would be
To change my ways, adapt my easy creed
  To suit to-morrow's need,
And pass my quiet days in long content.

I cannot think clearly now: [*Strophe* 2
I have seen a thing that I never thought to see, –
I have seen the brightest star of the city of Athens
Driven out by his father's anger
To look for another country.
Sandy shore fringing the city-wall,
You will not see him now ;
Nor you, oak-forests of the mountain-side,
Where in the train of the immortal Huntress
He followed with swift-footed hounds to make his kill!

We shall not see him now [*Antistrophe* 2
Leap up behind his trained Thessalian team,
Holding the smooth track round the shore-marshes
Breathless with the tense drumming of hooves.
The music that sang unsleeping from the plucked string
Shall be dumb in his father's palace.
The garlands will wither now
That you strewed in the deep Spring grass
Where Artemis loved to rest;
And the jealous war of girls who longed for your love,
Now you are gone, sinks into hopeless peace.

To me, Hippolytus, your fate has left [*Epode*
A life unreal, empty of all but tears.
    Dead are the dreams that lit
    Your mother's pains with joy.
Gods immortal, mortal rage reproaches you!
    How, you sister Graces,
Can you see him hounded from his father's home,
    Innocent, and outcast –
    Righteous, and uprooted?
CHORUS: Look! Someone is running this way! It is one of
   Hippolytus' men! And his eyes are full of horror!
                  Enter MESSENGER.

MESSENGER: Women, where can I find the King? Where is Theseus? If you know, tell me. Is he indoors?

CHORUS: Here is the King. He is coming out now. *—INTRO.*

Enter THESEUS.

MESSENGER: Theseus, I bring grave news – grave both for you and for all your people, whether of Athens or of Troezen.

THESEUS: What is your news? Can yet another calamity have fallen upon our two cities?

MESSENGER: Hippolytus is dead – or dying. His life hangs in the balance.

THESEUS: Who struck him? Was it the vengeance of some man whose wife he had dishonoured as he did his father's?

MESSENGER: It was his own chariot that killed him – and the curses which your lips called down from your father the sea-god upon your son.

THESEUS: By the gods! – so you have proved a true father to me, Poseidon: you heard my curse! And how did it happen? Tell me! How did the trap of justice close on the man who shamed me?

MESSENGER: We were on the shore, near the water's edge, combing down the horses and smoothing their manes; and we were weeping, for we had been told that Hippolytus was no longer free to come and go in Troezen, but was condemned by you to the miseries of exile. He came to us there, bringing the same tale of tears; and a great troop of friends and followers, young men like himself, came with him. After some time he stopped weeping and said to us, 'This is folly; my father must be obeyed. Men, yoke my horses, harness them to the chariot. This is not my country any more.' Then every man of us came with a will, and sooner than you could say it we had the team harnessed and standing ready at the prince's side. He caught up the reins from the driving-rail, and, dressed as he was for hunting, took his stand on

the chariot. And first he held up his hands and prayed:
'Zeus, may I die if I am a guilty man! And may my father
know how he has wronged me, – if not while I live, then
after I am dead!'

And now he had gripped the goad and was urging his
horses; and we servants began running beside the bridles, to
escort our master along the straight road to Argos and
Epidauria. We sped on, across the Troezenian frontier, and
reached a deserted part of the coast, beyond which, as you
know, a beach runs down to the Saronic Sea. It was there
that we heard a heavy rumbling sound, like the thunder of
Zeus, but rising out of the earth, with a deep roar that was
horrible to hear. The horses pricked their ears, lifted their
heads. We youths were terrified, wondering where the
sound came from. We looked out to the breaking surf, and
there we saw a wave of unearthly size, rearing to the sky;
it hid from my view not only the Scironian headland but the
Isthmus and the Rock of Asclepius. Then, swelling still
huger, and spattering foam on every side, it rushed seething
and hissing to the shore, and straight towards the chariot
and the four horses. And in the very moment of bursting and
crashing, the wave threw forth a monstrous savage bull,
whose bellow filled the whole earth with an appalling echo,
while the sight of him was too tremendous for mortal vision.
The horses were seized with a frenzy of terror. Hippolytus,
using his long experience in the ways of horses, gripped the
reins, twisting them round behind his back and dragging on
them as a rower tugs on his oar. It was no use: the beasts
took the wrought-iron bits between their teeth and careered
on, as though the driver's hand and the reins and harness
and the heavy chariot were nothing at all! When he struggled
to steer their hurtling course up towards the soft grass,
there was the bull in front to craze them with terror and
turn them back; when they went madly tearing towards the
rocks, then the bull kept close beside them, silent, and

swerving right in upon the chariot, until the moment when
he crashed the boss of the wheel against a rock and flung the
chariot tossing in the air. Then there was wild confusion –
wheels, axle, bolts, and frame leaping high. Hippolytus,
tangled in the reins, strung fast in an inextricable knot, was
dragged along, his head dashed on the rocks, his flesh torn;
while in a voice terrible to hear he shouted to his horses,
'Stop! You were reared in my own stables – will you grind
me to death?' Then he cried, 'Father, why did you curse
me? I am innocent! Will no one come to help me?'

Indeed, there were many of us willing enough, but run
as we might we were left behind. At last – how I do not
know – he fell clear of those fine reins that bound him. He
still breathed; though there was little life left in him. The
horses had vanished away over the rocky ground, I cannot
tell where; so had that dreadful prodigy of a bull.

My lord: I am only one of your palace slaves; but I never
can nor will believe that your son was guilty of so terrible
a crime – no, not if the whole race of women hanged themselves, not if a mountain of letters were written to accuse
him: I know that Hippolytus is a good man.

CHORUS: The wheel has turned; disaster follows disaster.
Fate is inevitable; there is no escape. *PHILOSOPHY*

THESEUS: Because I hated the man who has suffered this, I
was glad when I heard it; but remembrance of the gods
awes me: Hippolytus is my own flesh. What has happened
gives me neither pleasure nor grief.

MESSENGER: What shall we do? Shall we bring him to die
here? Or what would please you? Consider: your son is
struck down. Listen to my advice and do not be harsh to
him.

THESEUS: Bring him. Let me see face to face the man who
denies that he dishonoured my bed; so that my words and
the hand of heaven may convict him.

Exit MESSENGER.

CHORUS:
Aphrodite! You lead captive
Stubborn hearts of gods and mortals!
At your side with glinting wing
Eros, round his victim swiftly circling,
Hovers over earth and the salt sea's clear song.
When on the maddened spirit
He swoops with sweet enchantment,
Whelps of the mountain know the power of his golden wing;
Fish, and the unnumbered beasts that draw
Life from the earth's breast, warmth from the sun's eye, –
Yes, and the hearts of men,
Yield to the universal spell.
Aphrodite, you alone
Reign in power and honour,
Queen of all creation!

THESEUS *and the* CHORUS *are facing the statue of* APHRODITE;
ARTEMIS *appears beside her own statue on the other side of the*
stage. As she speaks all turn towards her.

ARTEMIS:
Theseus, royal son of Aegeus! I command you,
Listen! It is Artemis, Leto's daughter, who speaks.
Why do you, wretch, rejoice at what you have heard?
You have most sinfully murdered your own son.
You believed your wife's lies without witness: now
Witness the world how you reap your own undoing!
Will you not cower shamed in the depths of hell?
Soar to the sky to escape this chain of misery?
In the common life of good men
There is no place for you now.
She moves to centre of stage.

I will tell you, Theseus, the true state of your unhappy
life; and my words will not smooth your path, but sharpen
your pain. My purpose in coming is to disclose, first, your
son's uprightness of heart, that he may die with a good

name; then, your wife's frenzy – or, in some sense, her
nobleness. Phaedra, plagued and goaded by that goddess
whom I, and all who love virginity, most hate – Phaedra
loved your son. Reason struggled to subdue passion. She
died through schemes plotted against her will: her nurse
told Hippolytus, under oath of secrecy, the Queen's afflic-
tion. He honourably resisted her persuasions; even when
you so wronged him, still for reverence of the gods he
would not abjure his oath; but Phaedra, in terror lest she
be exposed, wrote that lying letter and by fraud killed your
son – yes, for you believed her!

THESEUS: My son, my son!

ARTEMIS: Do my words hurt, Theseus? Listen further, for you
have more to suffer. You know that your father promised
you the fulfilment of three curses? The first you have most
wickedly misused, cursing your son when you might have
cursed an enemy. Your father the sea-god gave all that he
was bound to give. He had promised; and the folly was
not his. Now in his eyes and in mine you are condemned.
Instead of waiting for proof, or prophetic guidance, giving
no room for question or the slow scrutiny of Time, with
unrighteous haste you flung your curse and killed your son.

THESEUS: Goddess, let me die!

ARTEMIS: Your sin is great. Yet even you may still find pardon
for what you have done. For it was Aphrodite who, to
satisfy her resentment, willed that all this should happen;
and there is a law among gods, that no one of us should seek
to frustrate another's purpose, but let well alone. I tell you,
but that I fear Zeus and his laws, I never would have submitted to such dishonour, as to stand by and see Hippolytus
go to his death; for he was dearest to me of all mortals.
You did not know the truth: this, first, frees your fault
from the deepest guilt. Then, your wife by her death pre-
vented any test of what she alleged, and thus made sure that
you would believe her. So this flood of misfortune has burst

chiefly upon you; but I too suffer. For a good man's death
is no joy to the gods; but the impious man we utterly
destroy, and his house and children with him.

CHORUS:

Ah, look! Here comes the piteous prince,

His young flesh torn, his fair head bruised.

Ah, suffering house! The hand of heaven has struck

Twice in one day, accomplishing

The heavy doom of your appointed pain.

Enter HIPPOLYTUS, *supported by huntsmen.*

HIPPOLYTUS:

Weep for me, weep for me,

Scarred, broken, trampled under foot

By man and god alike unjust, –

My father's curse, Poseidon's power;

Weep for my death!

My forehead is pierced with the fierce pain,

My brain convulsed with the pulse of anguish.

Enough now! I am fainting; let me lie.

They lay him down.

O horses my own hand fed,

Your cursed strength has crushed the breath from my body,

Torn the life from my limbs!

Men, for God's sake have careful hands

And touch me gently where the flesh is raw.

Who stands at my right side?

Lift me softly, with a steady grip.

Fallen cursed by my father's fault –

Zeus, do you see my agony?

I, that revered the gods with a holy heart,

I that was first in innocence,

Tread my way from life to the dark world,

And Death's eyes meet me as I go.

In vain I strove with patience

To love and serve my neighbour:
Now pain sets painful foot upon my body.
Let go, hold me no longer,
But let Death come to heal me;
And, if you pity me, help me to die quickly!
I am in love with the rending spear: come, cruel edge,
Shatter my heart and lull my life asleep!
Now, through my father's fatal curse,
The hellish heritage of bloodguiltiness
Won by forgotten ancestors
Descends impatient to the appointed heir –
On me it falls! Why? Why? I have done no wrong!
What shall I say? How can I ease my soul
And reach the end of anguish?
　　Lay me deep for evermore,
　　Death, with sore unyielding hand,
　　In the land of night and sleep!

ARTEMIS: Poor soul, galled with a bitter yoke! It was your noble heart that destroyed you.

HIPPOLYTUS: Ah, breath of divine fragrance! Goddess, I hear you, and my torment lightens. Is it truly Artemis, here in this place?

ARTEMIS: Poor soul, it is. You have no better friend among the gods.

HIPPOLYTUS: Lady, you see how it is with me?

ARTEMIS: I see; but my eyes are forbidden to shed tears.

HIPPOLYTUS: No one now to attend you in the hunt. . . .

ARTEMIS: No: you were my dear attendant; and you are dying.

HIPPOLYTUS: None to graze your horses, or guard your statues.

ARTEMIS: The wicked craft of Aphrodite has done this.

HIPPOLYTUS: Aphrodite! So, I know what god has killed me.

ARTEMIS: She resented your neglect and hated your purity.

HIPPOLYTUS: It is clear to me now: she has destroyed us all three.

ARTEMIS: You, and your father, and your father's wife.

HIPPOLYTUS: Though my father wronged me, yet I weep for him.

ARTEMIS: He was deceived: a god had planned it so.

HIPPOLYTUS: Father, how you have suffered to-day!

THESEUS: My son, my heart is broken; life is loathsome to me.

HIPPOLYTUS: Though the fault was yours, I weep for you more than for myself.

THESEUS: Would God I might die for you, my son!

HIPPOLYTUS: You too had little joy of your father's gifts.

THESEUS: O that that curse had never passed my lips!

HIPPOLYTUS: Why? You would have killed me, you were so angry then!

THESEUS: I was cheated by the gods out of my right mind!

HIPPOLYTUS: Oh, if only a man's curse could touch a god!

ARTEMIS:
You need not curse. Not even the black depths
Beneath the earth shall thwart the vengeance due
For this cruel wrong that Aphrodite's rage
Wreaked on your body for your pure soul's sake.
I will requite her: with this unfailing bow
My own hand shall strike down in just return
The man her heart holds dearest in the world.

On you, poor youth, I will bestow a place
Of highest honour in the city of Troezen.
The unmarried virgins shall, before their marriage,
Cut off their hair for you; age after age
Harvest of tears and mourning shall be yours,
Music of maidens' sorrow for your death.
And Phaedra too shall give her name to memory,
And songs shall celebrate her love for you.

C*

Theseus, remember your own father Aegeus:
Embrace your son and clasp him to your heart.
His death was not your will: men may well sin,
When the gods so ordain.

                              Hippolytus,
You must not hate your father; you know now
The destiny which has destroyed your life.
Farewell: I may not look upon the dead,
Nor stain my sight with death's last agony;
And now I see that you are near your end.

HIPPOLYTUS:

Farewell, immortal Virgin! Easy it is
For you to sever our long fellowship.
Since you desire it, I forgive my father,
As in days past I have obeyed your word.
Ah!
Darkness is closing now over my eyes.
Father, take hold of me; lift me upright.

THESEUS: What is it, dear son? Will you break my heart?

HIPPOLYTUS: I stand before Death's gates; I see them open.

THESEUS: And will you leave me guilty and defiled?

HIPPOLYTUS: No, no! I here absolve you of my death!

THESEUS: What? You will free me from the stain of blood?

HIPPOLYTUS: I swear it by the conquering bow of Artemis.

THESEUS: Dear son, how noble a heart you show your
    father!

HIPPOLYTUS: Pray that your true-born sons may be like
    me!

THESEUS: O generous soul, dying in innocence!

HIPPOLYTUS: Farewell, my father! Farewell, and farewell!

THESEUS: Do not forsake me now! Courage, my son!

HIPPOLYTUS:

My time for courage is past. I am gone, Father.
Cover my face now quickly with my cloak.
                    He dies.

THESEUS:

> Land of Athens, frontiers of a famous city!
>> When was man more noble?
>> When was loss more bitter?
> Aphrodite! with what endless tears and anguish
>> Shall your cruel contriving
>> Haunt my heart for ever!

CHORUS:

> Grief unlooked-for now fills every heart alike;
>> Tears from all eyes falling
>> Shall make mournful music.
> He was noble: loudly then from every tongue
>> Praise and lamentation
>> Through the world shall echo!

DEIFICATION

IPHIGENIA IN TAURIS

*

Characters:

IPHIGENIA, *daughter of Agamemnon*
ORESTES, *her brother*
PYLADES, *his cousin and friend*
THOAS, *King of the Taurians*
HERDSMAN
MESSENGER
The Goddess ATHENE
CHORUS *of captive Greek women attending Iphigenia*
SOLDIERS *attending Thoas*

*

Scene: The forecourt of the temple of Artemis on the Taurian coast, near the western end of the Crimean Peninsula. An altar is visible.

Enter IPHIGENIA *from the Temple.*

IPHIGENIA:

I am Iphigenia. I am descended
From that fast charioteer, the son of Tantalus,
Pelops, who drove to Pisa and there won
His wife Hippodamia. From them sprang Atreus;
From Atreus, Menelaus and Agamemnon.
He was my father; my mother, Clytemnestra.

The story's told how, in that land-locked bay
Of Aulis, where swift-eddying gusts of wind
Ceaselessly churn the dark swirl of Euripus,
My father slaughtered me, for Helen's sake,
A sacrifice of blood to Artemis.
For Agamemnon had assembled there
A thousand Grecian ships of war, resolved
To crown Greek arms in triumph over Troy,
Take vengeance for Helen's ravishing, and restore

Honour to Menelaus. But no wind
Stirred any sail. Disastrous calm drove him
To augury; and Calchas thus pronounced:
'Agamemnon, Marshal of the arms of Greece,
You shall see no ship sail till Artemis
Receive your daughter's blood in sacrifice.
Once, long ago, you vowed to Artemis,
Bringer of Light, the loveliest creature born
Within twelve months. This vow you did not pay.
Your own wife Clytemnestra has a child' –
(Thus singling out my beauty for the prize):
'Her you must offer.' So, by Odysseus' craft,
They stole me from my mother, giving out
That I was destined as Achilles' bride.
I came to Aulis. There they held me high
Over the pyre. The pitiless sword fell.
But, in that breath, Artemis came unseen
And took me from their hands; left in my place
A deer, and carried me through the bright air
To make my home here in this Taurian land,
Where Thoas rules, an uncouth king over
A race uncouth. His name is a runner's name,
Well earned, for his feet are swift as a bird's wing.

Here in this temple the divine Artemis
Made me her priestess; and at her will alone
I celebrate those ritual holy-days
She takes delight in – ceremonies pure
Only in name –: for dread of Artemis
I tell no more. The ancient law of the land
Demands for sacrifice every male Greek
Who sets foot on the Taurian coast. These victims
I first prepare for offering; others then
Lead them to the unspoken rite of slaughter
In the inmost chamber of this holy shrine.

Last night brought me strange dreams: I'll purge them forth
In words now to the sky, to ease my heart.
I dreamt I had escaped out of this land
And lived in Argos. There I and my maidens
Were sleeping, when the earth's shoulders heaved and shook.
I flew outdoors, and stood and watched the house –
Plinth, pillar, coping, roof – reel at one blow
And crash to earth. Out of the ruin which
Had been my father's house one column stood;
And from its head flowed golden hair; it spoke
With human voice. And I performed for it
My murderous rite for strangers, sprinkling water
As though on one destined to die, – and weeping.
What are the pillars of a house? Its sons!
And those my pure ablution touches die!
The dream, then, must mean this: it was Orestes
Whom I prepared for death; and he – has died.
So now I will make funeral offerings
For my dead brother – all I have power to do,
Being so far away. My maids must help –
Women of Greece the King appoints to serve me.
They should be here: what keeps them? I'll go in
To Artemis' temple, which I call my home.

IPHIGENIA *goes into the temple. Enter* ORESTES *and* PYLADES
from the shore. ORESTES *is depressed and nervous;* PYLADES
quiet and steady.

ORESTES: This is a path! Look out, make sure there is no
one –

PYLADES: I'm keeping my eyes open; I've looked all round.

ORESTES: Pylades! Is this the temple of Artemis, do you
think? the place we have crossed the sea from Argos to find?

PYLADES: Yes, I think so, Orestes. Don't you?

ORESTES: And the altar that flows with Greek blood?

PYLADES: Yes. Why, look! those dark stains round the edge –
they are blood!

ORESTES: And those are spoils hanging there, high up under the coping!

PYLADES: Trophies of visitors who died here!

ORESTES: Well, we must keep a good watch all round. – O Apollo! at your command I avenged my father's blood by killing my mother: now your divine word has led me into this new net – and where is it all to end? Hounded to exile by leash after leash of fresh Furies, an outcast from my home, haled and harried this way and that, – I have suffered my share! I came to you and asked how I might reach the end of this whirling madness that pursued me with torment through the length and breadth of Greece. You told me to come to this country, where your sister Artemis has her altars, and to take the statue of the goddess, which is said to have fallen from heaven here into this temple – to take it by craft or luck in face of all danger, and then to present it to Athens. No further command was given me; and, this once done, I was promised respite from suffering. I have obeyed you. Here I am, in an unknown and unwelcoming country.

Pylades, you must advise me, since you share the enterprise with me. What are we to do? You see how high the temple wall is. Are we to get in by climbing? We could hardly escape being seen. Or we might bring crowbars to loosen the bronze bolts – but we have no idea how they're fitted. If we're caught opening the doors, or breaking in by any means, we shall be killed. Let's get away, back to the ship we came in, while we're still alive!

PYLADES: No! Running away's out of the question. Besides, it's not our habit. We are doing a god's bidding, and we can't play the coward. But let us leave the temple now, and hide among those caves where the dark tide floods through the clefts – well away from the ship, in case someone sees it and informs the authorities and we find ourselves attacked and captured. Then, when night frowns over the gloomy

world – why, then we must use all the boldness and in-
genuity we have to steal that carved image out of the
temple. – Yes, look: between those blocks under the coping,
there's a hollow wide enough to climb through. Come!
difficulties show a good man's nerve; but a coward is a
failure anywhere. Why, surely we have not rowed all this
way only to set off home again as soon as we've reached our
goal!

ORESTES: You are right; I must listen to you. We must find
some spot here where we can safely hide. As you say, this
is Apollo's undertaking: he cannot wilfully allow his own
revealed purpose to fall to the ground. Bold is the word!
We are young – no difficulty can excuse us.

They steal away towards the shore. Enter the CHORUS.

CHORUS:
Keep holy silence, all whose homes
Are here, fringing the Unfriendly Sea,
Beyond the channel of the Clashing Rocks!

Huntress daughter of Leto,
Artemis of the mountains,
Into your maiden court I come,
Virgin slave to your temple's virgin guardian;
With pure feet pass
Between towering pillars, under the golden roof.

My home is far away,
Where by the cool Eurotas
Horses of Hellas crop the green meadows
Between the town wall and the shady river-bank:
There stood my father's house.

IPHIGENIA *appears from the temple.*

Mistress, we have come. – Oh, what has happened? Why are
you sad?
Daughter of great Agamemnon

Who led the famous fleet to the towers of Troy,
Ships and armed men by thousands and tens of thousands,
    Why did you call us to the temple?
    Why did you send for us?

IPHIGENIA:

Women, I am sunk in tears and deep distress.
    For me music has turned to mourning,
    And songs to sadness.
For Death lays pain, pain on my inmost heart,
    Blow follows blow, fatal and cruel:
I weep for the lost life of my own brother!
Such a sight I saw, such a vision came to me
    In the night whose darkness has just passed.
My life is shattered and ended: my father's house fallen,
    My family extinct!
O city, city of Argos, how you have suffered!
    Hear me, you Gods and Fates!
Why must you rob from me and send down to death
    My only brother?

Now I will rest his soul
With wine and water poured out on the earth's back,
Milk from the spilling udders of the mountain herd,
Liquor of ripe grapes, toil of the tawny bees –
The cup of the dead, set for the soothing of the dark Powers.

    Now give me the golden bowl
    And the offering for the God of Death.

    Child of Agamemnon's race,
    Numbered with the dead below,
    Take these holy gifts from me!
    I can lay no lock of hair,
    Drop no tear, upon your tomb.
    From the land that bore us both

Fate has torn me far away;
There men saw me slaughtered,
There men think me buried.

CHORUS:

Mistress, we will echo your chant of mourning
    With Eastern songs, with wild laments,
    Music to move tears for the dead,
        Notes the glad heart abhors,
The solemn dirge that Death himself intones.

The heir to Atreus' throne is dead,
    Hope of the royal house is dead!
Many a glorious king has Argos known:
    Whose is now the sovereignty?
Blow after blow crushes the cursed city,
    Since that first wickedness, at which
The Sun, driving winged horses like whirling flames,
    Swerved from his course, and averted
    The holy glance of his glory.
Agony upon agony, murder upon murder, dread and despair,
Attending the fatal talisman of the Golden Lamb,
        Haunted the unhappy house.
Now for the sons of Tantalus killed in time past
    Falls vengeance on the last of his line:
What God should frustrate, God against you fulfils!

IPHIGENIA:

God from the first for me fulfilled what he should not.
From the very night my mother loosed her maiden girdle,
From the hour I was conceived, over my childhood
        The hand of Fate lay hard.
    My unhappy mother, Leda's daughter,
    Whom many princes of Hellas wooed,
Gave birth to me as first fruit of her marriage –
    A doomed victim of my father's villainy,
    An offering not of joy but of terror:

For this she bore me, for this she fed and reared me!
  My life was forfeit by my father's vow:
They brought me in a chariot of state to the sands of Aulis,
A mocked and unblessed bride for Achilles son of Thetis!

Now, an exile at the bleak world's end
  Beside the Inhospitable Sea –
The Argive Hymn to Hera is not for me,
  Nor husband, child, city, nor friend;
Not for me to weave in patterned thread
  Athene's triumph and the Titans' doom,
  Lulled by the music of the loom;
But to perform dark rites unfit for song,
To drench an altar with the blood of the dead,
  To hear their piteous cries,
  To see the tears they shed,
  And stifle pity for their wrong!

Now to forget these horrors; for my tears
Yearn towards Argos, where my brother lies.
I left him a little child, so fresh, so young;
There in our mother's lap, fed by her breast, and kept
  Secure from unknown fears
  By her enfolding hands,
The infant heir of Argos' throne and lands,
  The young Orestes, slept!

CHORUS: Look, here comes a herdsman, my lady, from the
  shore! He has news for you.

HERDSMAN [*entering hurriedly*]: Daughter of Agamemnon and
  Clytemnestra! Listen to the news I have for you!

IPHIGENIA: Well, what is it that excites you so?

HERDSMAN: Two young men, my lady, have brought a ship
  safely through the channel of the blue Symplegades and
  landed here. The divine Artemis will be delighted with

them as victims for sacrifice! You must get ready the holy water and barley-meal at once, as quickly as possible.

IPHIGENIA: Men of what race? What country?

HERDSMAN: They are Greeks: I know that, but no more.

IPHIGENIA: Can you tell me their names? Did you hear them?

HERDSMAN: Yes; one of them called the other Pylades.

IPHIGENIA: And the first, his companion – what was his name?

HERDSMAN: No one knows that; we didn't hear it.

IPHIGENIA: Tell me how you saw them, how you met and captured them.

HERDSMAN: It was on the very edge of the dangerous sea, where the surf breaks –

IPHIGENIA: Oh? What business had you herdsmen down by the sea?

HERDSMAN: We had come down to wash the cattle in the salt water.

IPHIGENIA: Very well. Now begin again, and tell me what I want to hear – how you captured them. They have been long in coming. The altar of Artemis is not yet stained too red with the flow of blood from Greece.

HERDSMAN: We had brought our beasts down from the woodland pastures and were driving them into the sea which flows in through the Symplegades. There is a cave there carved out by huge waves bursting through, used as a shelter by purple-fishers; and here one of our drovers saw the two men, and made his way back to us on tip-toe. 'Do you see?' says he, 'those are gods sitting there!' One of us, a godfearing man, turned towards them and held up his hands and prayed, 'Lord Palaemon, son of the sea-nymph Leucothea, Protector of ships, if it be you, be gracious to us! Or if you are the Twin Brethren sitting there, or beings beloved by Nereus the father of the fifty immortal sea-nymphs – be gracious!' But another, a profane reckless

fellow, laughed at his prayer, and said they were ship-
wrecked sailors who had heard of the custom of this country
to sacrifice strangers, and were cowering under the rocks
in terror. Most of us agreed that he was right, and that we
ought to catch them to offer to Artemis according to
custom.

Just then one of the two started up from the rock he
sat on, and stood and jerked his head up and down and
groaned aloud, raving mad, with his hands trembling; and
he hallooed like a huntsman, 'Pylades, do you see her? and
look, another, a foul fiend from hell! Can't you see her?
all fanged with adders and coming at me to kill me! And the
third! with blood-red fire flaming from her skirts, fanned
with the beat of her wings! In her arms she holds a mountain
of stone to cast at me and crush me – it is my mother's
body! She is killing me! Where can I escape?'

Of course there were no such sights to be seen; but the
cattle were bellowing and the dogs barking, and he mistook
this for the shrieks and cries the Furies are supposed to give.
We sat silent, crouching in fear of death; when suddenly
he drew his sword and leapt like a lion right among our
cattle, lunging out and stabbing them in flank and rib,
imagining that he was fighting off the Furies – till the very
sea flowered with bloody foam.

Well, when we saw the poor beasts being felled and
slaughtered, every man of us got himself some weapon; we
blew our horns for help, and collected all the men within
call; we were only herdsmen, and we thought ourselves a
poor match for those two, young and strongly built. Before
long there was a good handful of us.

By this time the stranger had shaken off the violence of
his madness, and fell down, dribbling foam over his beard.
When we saw him fall, we took our chance, every one of us,
and pelted and struck with all our might. The second man
was wiping the foam from his friend's lips and supporting

his body and shielding him with the fine cloak he wore, watching against the rain of blows and still tending and soothing his friend. And now the first had recovered his right mind. He leapt to his feet; and seeing enemies advancing against them like a wave, he recognized that their fate was upon them, and shouted aloud. We were steadily advancing and throwing stones from all directions; and then we heard his terrible battle-call: 'Pylades, we shall die: so we must die nobly! Draw your sword and follow me!'

When we saw their two swords brandished at our heads, we scattered over the rocks and up the glens; but while some were running away, others were attacking with showers of stones; and when they routed these, those who had fled rallied and renewed the attack. And here was a thing hard to believe: of all the countless stones we threw, not one struck home, or scarred the victims destined for Artemis!

Well, at last we managed to lay hands on them, not so much by bravery as by closing round them in a circle till we knocked the swords out of their hands with stones, and they sank to their knees in exhaustion. Then we took them to the King; as soon as he saw them he sent them to you for purification, and then – sacrifice! Yes, my lady, you used to pray for men such as these to be sent you as victims: if you kill men of this quality, Greece will make amends for your murder, and pay what she owes for the blood spilt at Aulis.

CHORUS: What an amazing story! Who can he be, this mysterious stranger who has come from Hellas to the Unfriendly Sea?

IPHIGENIA: Enough! Herdsman, go now and bring the men; the ceremonies here are my concern and I will attend to them.

Exit HERDSMAN.

O my suffering heart! In past days, Iphigenia, when you laid ritual hands on the bodies of Greeks, you were full of goodwill and pity for them, and gave freely the tears that were due to your own flesh and blood. But now my dream has told me that Orestes no longer lives; and my heart is hardened; and therefore, whoever you may be that have come here, you shall find me cruel!

They say that the unfortunate who have known happier days hate those more fortunate than themselves: friends, my own heart tells me how true that is. Yet Zeus never sent wind or ship to convey Helen my destroyer, or Menelaus, through the Symplegades to this shore, that I might take due vengeance and make a second Aulis for atonement here! Aulis! where Greeks took hold of me as though I were a calf to slaughter me, while my own father officiated as priest! [*She weeps.*] How can I ever forget that day? ever forget how again and again I reached out to touch my father's beard, clung to his knees; 'Father', I cried, 'this is a shameful marriage you have brought me to! At this moment, while you are killing me here, my mother and my friends at Argos are singing the wedding-song for me and the house is echoing with the flutes; and I am being done to death – by you! No prince of Peleus' house, but Prince of Hell was the husband your lying promise gave me, when you had me brought in state in a bridal car to wed with bloody death!'

When I left home, I hid my face behind my fine wedding-veil, and would not clasp my brother in my arms – and he is dead now. Nor would I kiss my sister's lips, for I was hot with blushes because I was going to Achilles' house. I should visit Argos again one day, I told them; and I would keep my kisses until then.

O Orestes, my brother! what beauty and dignity of life is lost to you by your death! what splendour of inheritance!

As for Artemis, I find her guilty of hypocrisy! Her purity! Any man who has touched blood or a woman in labour or a corpse, Artemis calls unclean and bars him from her altars;

yet she herself delights in these murderous sacrifices! No, no, it is impossible! Could ever Zeus beget and Leto bring forth such vile folly? It is no more true than the tale of Tantalus feasting the gods and regaling them with the flesh of a child – these things I do not believe. I believe that the men of this country, being murderers, impute their own savagery to divine authority. I do not believe that any god is evil!

Exit IPHIGENIA *into the temple.*

CHORUS:

Dim purple rock, where sea flows into purple sea, *[Strophe* 1
Gateway from Europe to the vaster East,
Where Io in her mad agony passed through,
From Argos flying to these friendless waters!
   Tell us, who are these men?
What river flows past their forsaken home?
   Eurotas, clear between green rushes?
   Or the holy stream of Dirce?
Why have they come? come to a sullen land
Where the altar of Artemis daughter of Zeus runs red
   And human blood splashes the pillars?

Was it the jealous search for wealth to   *[Antistrophe* 1
   exalt their home
That drove their sails racing before the wind,
That plashed their pinewood oars, two wings as one,
To bring home riches over the wide waters?
   Such hope is sweet to men:
Though it bring sorrow, it is not satisfied.
They wander over the waves, visit strange cities,
   Seeking a world of wealth,
All alike sure of achievement; yet
One man's aim misses the lucky moment,
   Another finds fortune in his lap.

Trace the journey they have made: [*Strophe* 2
Through the crags that close like jaws,
    Past the swell unsleeping
    Of the bay of Phineus,
Skimming, coastwise, Amphitrite's restless foam,
    Where the fifty Nereid maidens
    Dance and sing in circling chorus; –
    Bellied canvas, the cleft ripples
    Noisy round the turning rudder;
South wind, West wind urging onward night and day
    To the myriad whiteness
Of the sea-birds on that gleaming island beach
    Where Achilles fleet of foot
      Smoothed his course for running
      On the lonely shingle!

Would some wind from Troy bring hither   [*Antistrophe* 2
Leda's darling, fatal Helen!
    That my mistress, gladdened
    With her prayer's fulfilment,
Might on Helen's silken hair
    Sprinkle fresh the deadly offering,
    Lay bare *her* white throat for slaughter,
    Point the knife and take her vengeance! –
Welcome justice! Yet – O dearest news of all –
    If some ship from Hellas
Came to free me from this weary slavery!
    O my land, my father's home!
    Even in dream to see you now!
    There to taste, as long ago,
      Ecstasy of singing,
      Rich and poor together!

CHORUS:

    Look, they are coming – the double sacrifice,
    Fresh blood for the altar of Artemis,

Their hands fast in fetters. Keep silence, friends.
– The herdsman told no lie: here to the temple come
   The choicest manhood of Hellas!
Goddess, if such barbaric ritual
Pleases your heart, accept their offering!
   Though Grecian piety abhors
The savage rite this people's law commands.

Enter ORESTES *and* PYLADES, *guarded; also* IPHIGENIA,
from the temple.

IPHIGENIA: Come. My first care is that the holy office be performed in due order. Release their hands: they are now consecrated and must stand unbound. Go into the temple and prepare what is necessary and customary for this observance.

The guards go. IPHIGENIA, *alone with* ORESTES *and*
PYLADES, *gives a deep sigh.*

IPHIGENIA: You were once little children: who was your mother then? your father? Have you a sister? How sad for her to lose such a fine pair of brothers! Such things Fate holds in store – no one knows for whom. The ways of God move to an end we cannot see; the coming calamity is never revealed. Chance leads us astray and baffles us. O unhappy men! Tell me where you come from. You are the first to sail here for a long time; and you will be long from home – dead, and for ever!

ORESTES: Lady, whoever you are, why do you grieve like this, and make our approaching fate still more bitter for us? It is not wise for a man in sight of death to try to conquer his fear of death by looking for pity when there's no hope. He makes two evils of one: he is known for a fool, and he dies none the less. Let Fate take its course. We need no lament from you. We know very well what sacrifices you offer here.

IPHIGENIA: First tell me this: which of you is the one they say was named Pylades?

ORESTES: If you really care to know, it is he.

IPHIGENIA: What Greek city does he belong to?

ORESTES: What good would it do you, lady, to know that?

IPHIGENIA: Are you two brothers?

ORESTES: Brothers in love; but not by birth.

IPHIGENIA: And you, – what name did your father give you?

ORESTES: My name – my true name is Ill Fortune.

IPHIGENIA: That name chance gave you: tell me the other.

ORESTES: I will die unknown; then at least I shall be safe from insult. You shall sacrifice my body, not my name.

IPHIGENIA: Are you so proud? Why do you grudge me this? Will you not even tell me your city?

ORESTES: What would you gain from that? I am to die.

IPHIGENIA: I ask a favour: what makes you refuse it?

ORESTES: I am a citizen of famous Argos.

IPHIGENIA: In God's name tell me the truth! – You are from Argos?

ORESTES: Yes, from the once prosperous Mycenae.

IPHIGENIA: Why did you leave home? Were you banished?

ORESTES: Banished? In one sense, yes. It was my own will, – and it was not.

IPHIGENIA: You are from Argos! This is what I have longed for!

ORESTES: Then make the most of it. I have not longed for it.

IPHIGENIA: Would you tell me something I want to know?

ORESTES: Yes. It can add nothing to my misfortunes.

IPHIGENIA: Perhaps you know Troy, that the whole world talks of?

ORESTES: I wish I had never known the shadow of the name of Troy!

IPHIGENIA: They say it was taken and laid waste in war.

ORESTES: Yes, that is true.

IPHIGENIA: And has Helen gone back to Menelaus?

ORESTES: She has.

IPHIGENIA· Where is she?

ORESTES: In Sparta; happy with her husband, as before; but she brought a curse with her for one that I know.

IPHIGENIA: I too have an old account to settle with her. And I am not alone – all Hellas hates her.

ORESTES: Yes; my life too bears the mark of her marriages.

IPHIGENIA: And did the Greek army return, as report says?

ORESTES: Ha! There you ask me the whole story in one word.

IPHIGENIA: It is that story I want from you before you die.

ORESTES: If you want it, question me; I will answer.

IPHIGENIA: Did a certain priest ever come home from Troy – one Calchas?

ORESTES: They were saying in Mycenae that he was dead.

IPHIGENIA: Artemis, my thanks! – What news of Odysseus?

ORESTES: They say he is alive; but he has not reached home yet.

IPHIGENIA: I hope he never will: my curse on him!

ORESTES: Save your curse; his home is full of trouble.

IPHIGENIA: And Thetis's son Achilles – is he still alive?

ORESTES: No, dead; and his marriage at Aulis came to nothing.

IPHIGENIA: Nothing but treachery, as those who suffered know.

ORESTES: Who are you? By your questions, you know something of Greece.

IPHIGENIA: I am from Greece. My life ended there when I was a child.

ORESTES: Then naturally you long for news.

IPHIGENIA: And when the famous victory was won, what of the successful general?

ORESTES: Who? The one I knew had little success.

IPHIGENIA: The king they called Agamemnon, son of Atreus.

ORESTES: I don't know. Lady: no more questions about him!

IPHIGENIA: Don't refuse, but tell me, in God's name. It will give me pleasure to hear.

ORESTES: He is dead; and his death destroyed another life too.

IPHIGENIA: Dead? How? Oh, not dead? Oh! [*She weeps.*]

ORESTES: What is the matter? Are you related to him?

IPHIGENIA: The thought of his past greatness makes me weep.

ORESTES: His death was terrible. His own wife cut his throat.

IPHIGENIA: Oh! How horrible, how pitiful! for her no less than for him.

ORESTES: Now stop: ask me nothing more.

IPHIGENIA: Tell me just this: is his wife still alive?

ORESTES: No. Her son killed her; yes, her very son.

IPHIGENIA: O house of madness and misery! Why? Why?

ORESTES: In vengeance for his father, whom she killed.

IPHIGENIA: It was right, – yet it was wrong! It was just, yet –

ORESTES: Yet the gods have not rewarded his justice.

IPHIGENIA: Has Agamemnon any child surviving?

ORESTES: Only Electra. She is not yet married.

IPHIGENIA: And is anything said of his daughter who was sacrificed?

ORESTES: Nothing, except that she is dead.

IPHIGENIA: Which should I pity more, her or her father who killed her?

ORESTES: Her life was thrown away for a worthless woman.

IPHIGENIA: But the son – since his father's death does he live in Argos?

ORESTES: He lives – like an outcast – nowhere and everywhere.

IPHIGENIA: He lives! So much for my dreams! They lied; they meant nothing.

ORESTES: Why, of course dreams mean nothing; and the gods themselves, even those called prophetic, are no more to be trusted than dreams are. Their divine world is as chaotic as our mortal one. That cannot be helped: but the thing that galls a man is that, in full possession of his senses, by obeying the words of soothsayers he should plunge himself into a depth of ruin which must be suffered to be understood.

CHORUS: And what of us? We too know what sorrow is. We loved our parents; but where are they now? Are they alive or dead? Who can tell us?

IPHIGENIA: Listen: a thought has come to me. I want to help you and myself at the same time. Some good most often follows when the same plan suits everyone. Would you agree, if I save your life, to take a message to my friends in Argos, and to carry a letter? The letter was written for me out of pity by a prisoner once, who saw that it was not my hand that killed him, but the hand of the law, as Artemis judges to be right. Since then I have had no one who could go back to Argos with my message, and buy his life from me by taking my letter to one who is dear to me. You seem to be of good birth; you know Mycenae, and the people I am thinking of. Be saved, then! Your life is no mean reward for carrying one little letter. And since the law insists upon a victim, let your friend alone be sacrificed to Artemis.

ORESTES: Lady, I agree to all you have said, except one thing. To let my friend die would be more than I could bear. Our voyage, with its risks and consequences, is my undertaking; he came only to share what I had to endure. So it would be wrong for me to purchase favour with his life, and myself step clear of danger. Instead, give him the letter; he will take it to Argos and deliver it to your satisfaction. My life may be his who wants it. A man who will run his friend's neck into the noose and escape himself is a coward. And this man is my friend: his life is as dear to me as my own.

IPHIGENIA: O generous heart, so true in friendship! I know you are of noble blood! If only the one still living of my family may be like you! For I too, my friends, have a brother, – except that I do not see him. ... Well, since you wish it so, we will send your friend to take the letter, and you shall die. This is a strange eagerness for death that possesses you!

ORESTES: Whose dreadful duty will it be to offer me?

IPHIGENIA: Mine; entrusted to me by the goddess.

ORESTES: You have an unenviable and tragic office!

IPHIGENIA: I have no choice but to obey.

ORESTES: Do you, a woman, wield the sword and kill men with your own hands?

IPHIGENIA: No. I shall sprinkle water on your head for purifying.

ORESTES: And who will kill me? May I ask this?

IPHIGENIA: That belongs to others inside the temple.

ORESTES: What kind of grave will receive me when I am dead?

IPHIGENIA: The altar-fire in the temple, then a wide chasm in the cliff.

ORESTES: O gods! if only my sister might compose my body for burial!

IPHIGENIA: A hopeless prayer, poor soul, whoever you may be! She is a long way from this savage place. But, since you are a man of Argos, I certainly will not neglect to do for you everything that is possible. I will heap rich gifts over your burial-place, spill golden olive-oil to quench your ashes; and pour over your pyre the bright juice that yellow bees sip from hillside flowers.

I will go now and fetch my letter from the temple. Do not hate me! *I* am not your enemy. [*The guards re-appear.*] Guards, watch them, but leave them free. [*At the door she pauses, speaking to herself.*] He has no thought that I still live – he whom I love most dearly! Now, it may be, I shall send a message for him to Argos; my letter will tell him I am not dead, but alive; and give proof and certainty to his joy!

Exit.

CHORUS [*to* ORESTES]:
> Heart and soul I grieve for you:
>> Soon the holy drops
>> On your head will fall,
> Claim your blood and seal your death.

ORESTES: I do not ask for pity; so, farewell!

CHORUS [*to* PYLADES]:
> Pylades, we give you joy!
>> Fortune is your friend:
>> Soon your native shore
> Once again will welcome you.

PYLADES: Will you give joy to one whose friend is to die?

CHORUS I: Each must tread a cruel road.
      2:   Weep for him, so young to die!
      3:   Weep for him who lives bereaved!

CHORUS: Which is harder, life or death?
>> For which fate
> Should my grief cry louder,
> Must my tears flow faster?

ORESTES: By heaven, Pylades, have you the same thought that I have?

PYLADES: I don't know. [*Collecting himself.*] What do you mean?

ORESTES: Who is that woman? No one but a true Greek could have asked those questions about the war at Troy and the return of the army, and the old star-gazer Calchas! Then, to speak of Achilles by name, and to be so moved with pity at the tragic fate of Agamemnon – to ask about his wife and children! She must have been born there her-self, in Argos! or she would never be sending a letter, and asking those detailed questions, as if the welfare of Argos concerned her closely.

PYLADES: You have said what I was on the point of saying; – except for this: the story of the two kings is known in every land that anyone ever visits. No; there was something else that she said —

ORESTES: What? Something that puzzles you? Tell me.

PYLADES: It would be a disgrace for me to live while you die. I shared your voyage: it is for me to share your death. If I escape now, in Argos and the Phocian valleys they will call me traitor and coward. There is no lack of slanderers. Most men will assume, when I arrive home alone, that I saved my life by deserting you — even that I murdered you, that I took advantage of the troubles of your family and plotted your death for the sake of a throne, being, as your sister's husband, your clear successor. The thought fills me with fear and shame. There is no other way: I am your friend, and I am afraid for my honour; therefore I must breathe my last breath with you, and give my body with yours to the knife and the fire.

ORESTES: Say no such thing! My own fate I must accept; but when only one grief is laid on me I will not bear two. This shame and disgrace you speak of is mine, if I repay your comradeship with death. For myself, persecuted as I am by the gods, to die now is no disaster. But you are rich; and your house is pure and untainted, while I am a bloodguilty outcast. You will escape; and my sister, whom I gave you as your wife, will bear you children; my name will be carried on, and my father's house will not be blotted out for want of an heir. Go, and live, and take up your inheritance!

And when once again you see Hellas and the chariots of Argos, do this for me, which I solemnly lay upon you: build a tomb, and set on it a memorial of me, and let my sister come there to weep for me and dedicate a lock of her hair. Tell her that I died at the hands of an Argive woman, who consecrated me for sacrifice before an altar. And, Pylades, never desert my sister, when you see her family extinct and her house desolate.

Good-bye! We have hunted together, and grown up to-

gether; you have borne for me many of the burdens of my
wretched life; and you have been to me the dearest of my
friends. As for me, I die the dupe of Apollo's oracles: he
cunningly traded on my reverence for his former commands,
to drive me out of Greece to the ends of the earth. I obeyed
him, placed my whole life in his hands: I killed my mother –
and now it is my turn to die.

PYLADES: I will build your tomb; and I will never desert
your sister, for you will be dearer to me, Orestes, in death
than in life. But – near though you are to death, Apollo's
oracle has not destroyed you yet. Sometimes, somehow, it
chances that extraordinary misfortune takes some extraordinary turn.

ORESTES: Say no more. I put no hope in any words of
Apollo. – See! she is coming out.

Enter IPHIGENIA *from the temple.*

IPHIGENIA: Guards, go inside now and make everything
ready there for those who are to perform the sacrifice. [*To*
PYLADES.] Here is the letter, in this folded tablet. Now
attend to what I require further. A man facing death is never
the same man when fear has faded and confidence returns;
I am afraid lest the bearer of my letter to Argos, once safely
out of this country, may forget my commands.

ORESTES: What do you wish, then? Why do you hesitate?

IPHIGENIA: Let him give me his oath to carry this letter to
Argos and deliver it to the friend whom I shall name.

ORESTES: Then will you give him your oath in return?

IPHIGENIA: What shall I swear to do, or not to do?

ORESTES: To see him alive and safe out of this country.

IPHIGENIA: Of course; or how could he take my message?

ORESTES: Will your king consent to this?

IPHIGENIA: Yes. I will persuade him, and take Pylades on
board myself.

ORESTES [*to* PYLADES]: Swear. [*To* IPHIGENIA.] Tell him
what oath he may use without impiety.

IPHIGENIA: Say, 'I will give this letter to your friends'.

PYLADES: I will give this letter to your friends.

IPHIGENIA: And I will send you safely beyond the Purple Rocks.

PYLADES: Which of the gods do you take to witness your oath?

IPHIGENIA: Artemis, in whose temple I am priestess.

PYLADES: I swear by the majesty of Zeus, King of Heaven.

IPHIGENIA: And if you break your oath and fail me?

PYLADES: May I never reach home! And if you fail to save my life?

IPHIGENIA: Then may I not live to set foot in Argos again!

PYLADES: Wait! There is a point we have forgotten.

IPHIGENIA: There is still time to speak of it, if it is fair.

PYLADES: Grant me this provision: if my ship should be wrecked, and everything I have sunk in the sea, and your letter among the rest, and I escape only with my skin, then my oath shall not be binding.

IPHIGENIA: I will tell you what I will do to make doubly sure: I will say over to you now what is written in the letter, for you to repeat at length to my friends. So we shall be safe: if you preserve the letter, it will give its own silent message; if it is lost in the sea, and you are safe, my words will be safe with you.

PYLADES: That is the best way for us both. Tell me to whom I must take it in Argos, and the words I must learn by heart.

IPHIGENIA: Say this to Orestes, son of Agamemnon: 'This message is from Iphigenia, who was sacrificed in Aulis. Though dead to all her friends, she is alive.'

ORESTES: Alive? Then where is she? Has she come back from the dead?

IPHIGENIA: I am she, whom you see here. But you interrupt; let me speak. – This is her charge: 'Bring me home, my brother, to Argos before I die. Release me from my priest-

hood in this barbarous place, where I preside at the slaughter-
ing of strangers on the altar of Artemis –'

ORESTES: Pylades, what does she mean? Are we dreaming?

IPHIGENIA: '– or I shall haunt your house with a curse,
Orestes.' – I say the name again so that you may remember it.

PYLADES: O ye gods, ye gods!

IPHIGENIA: Why call on the gods? What is Orestes to you?

PYLADES: Nothing – my thoughts wandered. Go on! [*Aside
to* ORESTES.] If I ask no questions I shall probably get the
truth.

IPHIGENIA: Tell him that Artemis saved me from my own
father's hands; that the sharp sword with which he thought
he struck me fell instead on a deer which the goddess provided in my place; and that she then brought me to live
here. That is your charge; those are the words written in
my letter.

PYLADES: Oh, lady, you have bound me with an easy oath,
and given a fair promise in return. I'll lose no time in doing
what I swore to do. See! Orestes, I bring and deliver you
this letter from your own true sister!

ORESTES: I accept it – but what do I want with written
words? I have a nearer way to embrace this joy: my darling
sister! I am so crazed with astonishment that I can scarcely
believe what I hear – a happiness beyond hope! Yet let me
take you in my arms!

CHORUS: Stop! Take your hands away! You defile the sacred
robes! To touch them is sin.

ORESTES: My own sister, don't turn me away! We are both
Agamemnon's children! You have your brother back, whom
you never thought to see again!

IPHIGENIA: You my brother! You are absurd! He is well
enough known in Argos, and in Nauplia too.

ORESTES: My sister, *your* Orestes is not in Argos!

IPHIGENIA: And Clytemnestra of Sparta was your mother?

ORESTES: Yes, and my father the grandson of Pelops.

IPHIGENIA: Oh! ... Have you any proof of this?

ORESTES: Proof enough! Ask me questions about our family.

IPHIGENIA: Better, surely, for you to speak and for me to listen.

ORESTES: I'll speak first of things Electra told me. You know of the quarrel between Atreus and Thyestes?

IPHIGENIA: For the Golden Lamb – yes, I have heard.

ORESTES: You know that you wove the scene in fine tapestry?

IPHIGENIA: Dear brother, that touches me – I almost believe!

ORESTES: And you wove in your picture the sun turning back in the sky!

IPHIGENIA: Yes, that was in my tapestry too –

ORESTES: And your mother sent holy water to Aulis for your wedding?

IPHIGENIA: I remember. She sent it because I was to marry a prince.

ORESTES: What else? – Yes! You gave a lock of your hair to be brought to your mother.

IPHIGENIA: I did! Since she could not have my body, I sent her a token for my tomb.

ORESTES: And now a proof I have seen with my own eyes: hidden in your own room in our father's palace, that old spear which Pelops hurled when he killed Oenomaus at Pisa and won his daughter Hippodamia!

IPHIGENIA: O dearest brother! You must be – you are – my darling Orestes! I have found you – so far from home, from Argos! O my dearest!

They embrace each other.

ORESTES: We thought you were dead; and I have found you! Your eyes are wet, and mine are wet too; but our tears are streams of happiness, and our sobs are all joy!

IPHIGENIA:

You were so little when I said good-bye to you!
There at home I left you

Nestling helpless in your nurse's arms!
  What can I say to you?
I am happier now than any words can tell.
  Our strange story stretches
  Beyond all thought or wonder.

ORESTES: God grant we now find happiness together!

IPHIGENIA:
  O friends, I hold in my hand
  Such a miracle of delight,
  That I dread it may fly from my grasp,
  Escape like smoke to the sky!
  My own dear city, Mycenae,
  Altar and hearth of home,
Hear my rapture of thanks for your faithful care,
Thanks for your rugged girdle of Cyclops' walls,
Where you reared my own Orestes safe to the stature of
    man,
  A light of hope for his darkened house!

ORESTES: Sister, our city and our race are noble;
      But we – are cursed, and born to misery.

IPHIGENIA:
      Well I know, to my sorrow,
      How my unhappy father
      Raised the knife to my naked throat.

ORESTES: That pitiful sight is branded on my soul!

IPHIGENIA:
  No wedding-hymn was chanted,
  When treacherously they led me
  Decked as a bride for Achilles' bed,
And the altar of joy was ringed with tears and groaning,
And the ritual cleansing mocked with guilt.

ORESTES: How could my father do it? It breaks my heart!

IPHIGENIA:
  Had I a father? How can I call him father?
    So from each engendering crime

Fate leads us blindly on to deeper calamity –

ORESTES: How nearly my own blood had stained your hands!

IPHIGENIA:

What was I doing? Brother, how horrible!
    Could I have stood and seen you die?
        Oh! how slender a chance
Delivered you from death and me from bloody defilement!

And now, how will it end? Will luck be timely?
    What device of mine can help you
    Quit the land and cheat the altar,
    Leap the leagues from here to Argos,
Now, before the knife can taste your blood?
Think, my despairing brain! The way is for you to find!
By land, leaving the ship – trust to your heels?
You would die among savage tribes and trackless deserts.
    No, you must fly by ship,
Make for the Blue Strait and the Narrow Rocks –
A weary, endless journey – gods have mercy!
Oh, I am helpless, helpless! O my brother,
        What aid from earth or heaven,
        What miracle past hoping
        Could work the impossible,
    And save our lives, the last remaining
Glimmers of hope for the house of Atreus?

CHORUS: All this is stranger than any tale. If I had not seen
it with my own eyes I could not believe it.

PYLADES: Orestes, it is natural that you and your sister
should embrace each other on meeting after so many years;
but now you must put emotion aside and concentrate on
the one grand theme – Escape! Away from this savage
place to safety! When a good chance is offered, it is wise
not to flout Fortune by wasting time, however delight-
fully.

ORESTES: You are right. I think our deliverance lies as much

with Fortune as with ourselves; but if we play our part
Heaven will be the stronger on our side.

IPHIGENIA: But you shall not stop me from asking first about
Electra – any news of her is precious to me. Is she well?
What has become of her?

ORESTES: She is to be married to Pylades, and is very happy.

IPHIGENIA: And Pylades – what is his city, and who is his
father?

ORESTES: He is the son of Strophius King of Phocis.

IPHIGENIA: Then he too is related to me – a grandson of
Atreus?

ORESTES: Yes, he is your cousin; and my one tried friend.

IPHIGENIA: He was not born when my father led me to death.

ORESTES: No; it was some time before Strophius had any
child.

IPHIGENIA: My dear sister's husband – give me your hand!

ORESTES: He is more than cousin to me: I owe him my very
life.

IPHIGENIA: Tell me, Orestes, about our mother. How did
you bring yourself to such a terrible act?

ORESTES: Let us not speak of that. – I avenged my father.

IPHIGENIA: But why – why did she kill him?

ORESTES: Don't ask me about her. It is not for you to hear.

IPHIGENIA: I will not ask. And you are now lord of Argos?

ORESTES: I am an exile. Menelaus governs Argos.

IPHIGENIA: What? Did Menelaus choose our moment of
weakness to turn traitor?

ORESTES: No; it is the Furies I am afraid of. They drove me
out, and they still pursue me.

IPHIGENIA: Ah! Yes, they told me of your frenzy on the
shore.

ORESTES: It is not the first time men have witnessed what I
suffer.

IPHIGENIA: I understand: they torment you for our mother's
sake.

ORESTES: When they have me bridled, they drive till I drip blood.

IPHIGENIA: But what could have brought you to land on this coast?

ORESTES: Obedience to Apollo's oracle.

IPHIGENIA: What have you come to do? Are you permitted to tell me?

ORESTES: Yes. Listen: I'll tell you how all my sufferings began. When I found myself burdened with my mother's – with what I will not speak of –, the Furies drove me as a fugitive this way and that, until Apollo at last sent me to Athens to be brought to trial there by the Nameless Goddesses. For in Athens there sits an inviolable court, before which Zeus, they say, long ago summoned Ares on some charge of murder. When I arrived, at first every Athenian refused me shelter, as a man hated by the gods. Later, those who had some conscience allowed me to sit and eat alone at a separate table; I slept under the same roof with them; and without speaking a word to me they made signs that I was to eat and drink apart. They would pour out for me into a separate flagon the same measure of wine as for everyone else, and so enjoy their feast. Well, I thought it wise not to protest – they were my hosts. I swallowed my resentment, and with a bitter heart pretended not to know that I was a matricide. (And since then, they tell me, Athens commemorates my unhappy visit by a yearly festival which they call the Feast of Flagons.)

However, I appeared before the court of Areopagus. I stood on a dais on one side of the court, on the other stood the Eldest of the Furies, demanding justice for my mother's murder. I defended myself; but it was Apollo's evidence that saved me. Athene counted the votes, found them equal, and raised her hand for my acquittal: I had been tried for my life, and I had won. Thereupon those of the Furies who accepted the judgement established their permanent shrine in the court itself; those who rejected it continued still to persecute me from place to place, till at last I came again to Apollo's temple at Delphi. I lay at his door prostrate and starving, and swore I would leave my corpse rotting there unless Apollo, who had ruined me, would save me. Then the voice of the god pealed forth from the golden tripod, commanding me to come to this place, take the image of Artemis that fell from heaven, and set it up in Athens.

This was the way of deliverance he prescribed for me: help me to carry it out! Once we secure this image, I shall be free of my madness, escape with you to our ship, set sail for Mycenae and bring you to your home again. Sister, O my dearest sister, save our father's house, and save me from this altar! The holy image that fell from heaven – we must get it! or else I am a dead man, and the house of Pelops is dead too.

CHORUS: Surely some seething anger of gods has raged against the sons of Tantalus, dragging them from disaster to disaster!

IPHIGENIA: I was longing for Argos even before you came, and longing to see you again, Orestes; and I wish now for all that you desire, – to release you from suffering, to forget my resentment against my father, and help to retrieve the disasters that have fallen upon our family. Instead of killing you I must save your life, and so save us all.

But I am afraid of Artemis, whom we cannot deceive, and of the King, when he finds the stone pedestal there and the image gone. What plea could I make? It would be certain death. If only you can contrive to do these two things – to steal the statue and to bring me on board your ship – then it's well worth the risk. But if you cannot do both, then you must carry off the statue without me; and I must die, but you will succeed in your task and reach home safely. I am not afraid – no, not even of death, if I can save you. No family can afford to lose its men; but a woman can be of little use.

ORESTES: No! My mother's blood is on my hands – that is enough; I will not be your murderer as well as hers. I stay with you for life or death: either I escape and take you to Argos with me, or I die here with you. And think of this too: how can it be distasteful to Artemis that I should carry off her statue to Athens, when her brother Apollo has commanded me? Now I begin to see his purpose: he intended that I should find you here. I see many threads drawing together; I think we shall reach home!

IPHIGENIA: But how to do both things at one time, escape death and steal the image? That's where our hopes fall down; that is what we must plan.

ORESTES: Well: could we kill the King?

IPHIGENIA: It would be wrong. I am a foreigner and he is my host.

ORESTES: If it will save our lives we must risk that.

IPHIGENIA: No. It is a brave suggestion, but I could not.

ORESTES: What if you hid me in the temple?

IPHIGENIA: To wait for darkness and then escape?

ORESTES: Yes; night's the time for stealing. Daylight's too honest for me.

IPHIGENIA: The temple guards are inside; they would find us.

ORESTES: Heaven help us, then, we are lost. How can we escape?

IPHIGENIA: I think I begin to see another way.

ORESTES: Yes? Tell me!

IPHIGENIA: I could use your – misfortune to deceive the King.

ORESTES: Yes! That's like a woman's cleverness!

IPHIGENIA: I'll say you have come straight from murdering your mother at Argos; that the victim must be pure; that you are unclean and therefore unfit for sacrifice.

ORESTES: Yes, if it is of any advantage, use my disgrace. I

think I see the plan. – But how will this help in stealing the image? That's what we came to get, and it's still in the temple!

IPHIGENIA: I shall need to purify your body in the sea; and I shall say that the statue too must be cleansed, as you have touched it.

ORESTES: Cleansed – where? On the wet rocks of that headland –

IPHIGENIA: Where your ship's anchored! Yes!

ORESTES: Will you yourself carry the image, or someone else?

IPHIGENIA: I will. No one else is allowed to touch it.

ORESTES: And Pylades here – will you say he shared in the murder?

IPHIGENIA: I shall say that his hands are stained like yours.

ORESTES: What of the King? Will you do all this with his knowledge or without?

IPHIGENIA: He will have to know; but my story will convince him.

ORESTES: Well, my ship's ready, my crew only waiting to dip their oars.

IPHIGENIA: Yes, that part of the plan must be left to you.

ORESTES: One other thing: these women here must keep the secret. Speak to them, use all your persuasion – a woman's appeal is more moving. If they are loyal, the rest may go well enough.

IPHIGENIA *turns to the* CHORUS.

IPHIGENIA: Dear friends, my whole future now lies with you. It is for you to decide whether I shall live or die – whether I shall succeed, or lose for ever my country, my sister and my brother. And my first appeal is this – we are women: women have a feeling for one another, and can be trusted to share secrets and keep them. Say nothing of what we are doing, but help us to make good our escape! To have a tongue that your friend can trust is a noble thing. You see how a single chance will decide now for us three, who love each other dearly, between a safe home-coming and death. If I live, I will come and fetch you too back to Greece to share my good fortune. – [*She addresses them one by one.*] I ask you, I entreat you – and you, good friend – and you, my dear – and you, and you: remember our friendship; remember those that you have loved, your parents or children; and promise me your help! What do you say? Which of you is with me, or against me, in this? Speak now. If you reject my appeal, it is all over with me and with my brother.

CHORUS: Have no fear, dear mistress; only get safely away! You ask us to say nothing: then, by Almighty Zeus, not a word shall be spoken!

IPHIGENIA: The gods bless you for that promise and bring you happiness! Brother, Pylades, you must go into the temple; the King will be here immediately, to ask if the sacrifice has been performed.

　　　Artemis! In the bay of Aulis you saved me from my father's murderous hand: now once more, save me and save us all! or else bring mistrust and scorn upon the oracles of Apollo! Graciously come with us out of this savage land to Athens. Here is no fit place for your home: there a city of joy waits to welcome you!

Exeunt into temple.

CHORUS:

Lonely halcyon haunting the sharp sea-cliffs,　　　　　[*Strophe* 1
　　Threading the air with notes of pain –
　　Notes that can speak to those that know –
A ceaseless song calling your lost lover!
　　　　Bird of sorrow, hear me sing,
　　　　Wingless, but like you in grief
　　　　　For the folk of Hellas,
　　　　　The familiar faces!
Shapely laurel of Delos and soft-haired palm remembered,
　　Sacred olive silver-green,

Grove that befriended Leto's labour,
Shading the temple-porch beside the Cynthian hill,
Where they offer to Artemis not blood but blessing!
And, cool below the temple, the round lake,
    Where slow pools turn, and the still swan,
Melodious servant of the Muses, floats!

Then—my pale cheek wet with my tears' anguish: [*Antistrophe* 1
    Enemy spears — the shattered wall —
    Slaughter and capture! And we went
In chains to the conquering ships and across the sea.
        Bought for gold, my journey's end
        Brought me to this barbarous coast,
Where I am slave to Agamemnon's daughter,
        Priestess of Artemis, and serve
Before the altar that flows with Grecian blood.
    Happy are those who never knew
    Gladness, whose birth embraced misfortune,
Steeling their souls to endure adversity —
My still-remembering heart envies their stubborn will!
From joy to tears — this cruel exchange
Weighs down the mortal spirit with long despair.

    But you will escape to Argos,   [*Strophe* 2
With fifty oars, lady, to wing you home;
And the whistling waxen pipes of Pan-of-the-mountain
    Shall shrill to the rowers' rhythm;
    And the Prophet-Singer Apollo
Shall come with the Seven Chords of Song and escort you
    To the shining city of Athens!
        I shall stay and see you go,
        Watch the oar-blades' foamy track,
    Yard-arms bending, bellied sails and sheets astrain,
        As your ship flies onward
        Into the dim distance.

O path of the Sun's bright horses!   [*Antistrophe* 2
To follow that fiery splendour West and home!
I would fold impatient wings over weary shoulders
    By my own loved home of childhood!
    With yearning thoughts I remember
The weddings in noble houses, the whirl of dancing,
The bridesmaids singing together, and I among them,
In pride of youth and delicate ornament
    And glory of rival graces:
    Days when I was young and fair,
        When I still would shade
My maiden cheek with scarves of coloured braid,
        And with my curling hair!

Enter THOAS, *with guards.*

THOAS: Where is the Greek woman, the temple-guardian?
    Has she performed the proper ceremonies? And are the
    strangers' bodies now blazing on the altar?

CHORUS: King, she is coming herself, and will tell you every-
    thing.

Enter IPHIGENIA, *carrying the image of Artemis.*

THOAS: What! Daughter of Agamemnon! That is the image
    of Artemis in your arms! Why are you moving it from its
    inviolable place?

IPHIGENIA: King, stay where you stand, there by the pillars!

THOAS: Iphigenia, what has happened here?

IPHIGENIA: Happened? Nothing — we must avoid unlucky
    words!

THOAS: What is all this mystery? Will you tell me plainly?

IPHIGENIA: The two men that you caught — I found them
    unclean and not fit for sacrifice.

THOAS: Is that merely your opinion? What could make you
    sure of it?

IPHIGENIA: The holy image shrank backwards on its pedestal.

THOAS: Not of itself? Surely the earth trembled and moved it!

IPHIGENIA: Of itself. The image shook, and its eyes closed.

THOAS: What was the cause? Those men's pollution?

IPHIGENIA: That, and nothing else. They are guilty of fearful crimes.

THOAS: Perhaps they killed one of my men on the shore?

IPHIGENIA: No; they have brought their guilt here with them.

THOAS: You make me curious. What have they done?

IPHIGENIA: Those two men together killed their mother.

THOAS: Gods! Even a savage would shrink from that!

IPHIGENIA: They have been driven out of every city in Greece.

THOAS: I see now: this is why you are bringing the image –

IPHIGENIA: Out under the pure sky, for cleansing of blood.

THOAS: How did you discover their crime?

IPHIGENIA: When the image turned away, I questioned them.

THOAS: Ha! You understood! You Greeks are clever.

IPHIGENIA: These men are: they held out a bait to win my heart.

THOAS: Oh! Tempted you with news from Argos, no doubt?

IPHIGENIA: They brought me good news of my only brother Orestes, and told me my father too is alive and well.

THOAS: No doubt they hoped you would save them from death in return; instead you chose to perform your duty to Artemis – as is natural.

IPHIGENIA: I remember what Greece did to me: I hate all Greeks.

THOAS: But now tell me, what are we to do with these men?

IPHIGENIA: We must obey the established law.

THOAS: To work, then, with your holy water and your sword!

IPHIGENIA: First they must be purified; I must bathe them in water.

THOAS: In a fresh spring, or in the sea?

IPHIGENIA: The sea washes clean all human ills.

THOAS: Good: their death will be the more acceptable to Artemis.

IPHIGENIA: And what *I* have to do will also be better done.

THOAS: Well, here the surf breaks close by the temple.

IPHIGENIA: We must go to some lonely place; there are other rites to perform.

THOAS: Take them where you wish. I'll not pry into mysteries.

IPHIGENIA: I must purify the image too.

THOAS: If it is infected with the guilt of murder –

IPHIGENIA: If not, I would never have moved it from its place.

THOAS: Of course. Your piety and care are very proper.

IPHIGENIA: Now this is what I want: the men must be bound –

THOAS: As you say; but where could they escape to?

IPHIGENIA: Never trust a Greek!

THOAS: Guards, bring ropes!

IPHIGENIA: Let them bring the men out, and wrap their cloaks over their heads –

THOAS: They would defile the daylight!

IPHIGENIA: I shall need some of your guards.

THOAS: These men can go with you.

IPHIGENIA: And send a herald through all the streets –

THOAS: Yes?

IPHIGENIA: To tell everyone to remain indoors, to avoid all contact with guilty blood. Even to see would bring pollution.

THOAS: True, true. [*To an attendant.*] Go and give the order.

IPHIGENIA: Take especial care that no one dear to me –

THOAS: You are thinking of me, I know!

IPHIGENIA: – that no one catches sight of them.

THOAS: How well you guard my people!

IPHIGENIA: It is natural.

THOAS: And it is natural that everyone looks up to you.

IPHIGENIA: *You* must stay here at the temple and purge the whole building with fire.

THOAS: It shall be clean when you return. What else?

IPHIGENIA: When the men come from the temple, hold your cloak before your eyes to avoid any taint of guilt.

THOAS: I will.

IPHIGENIA: If I seem to be too long away –

THOAS: How soon shall I expect you?

IPHIGENIA: – there is no need to be disturbed.

THOAS: Take what time is necessary to perform the rites with due care.

IPHIGENIA: God grant this cleansing may succeed as I wish!

THOAS: God grant it!

The temple doors open.

IPHIGENIA: I see the men coming out of the temple now; and the attendants are bringing the image's sacred robes, and two young lambs, with whose pure blood I will wash away the blood of uncleanness, and burning lamps, and other holy emblems of purifying power which I have prepared for these tainted men and for the infected image.

She raises the image, and the procession forms.

I warn every man to keep far from the unholy thing; every temple-servant whose hands are consecrated; everyone who goes to-day to be joined in marriage; every woman with child: away, stand apart, lest this defilement fall upon any one of you!

Goddess, virgin daughter of Zeus and Leto, if I may purge these men's guilt, and thereafter pray to you in a place fit for prayer, you shall be housed in a pure temple, and we shall receive blessing! – The rest I pray, in thought and not in word, to the gods who know all things, and to you, my mistress, Artemis!

IPHIGENIA, ORESTES, PYLADES *and several guards go out towards the shore in solemn procession.* THOAS *and the remaining guards go into the temple.*

CHORUS:

   This is the story of the oracle of Apollo at Delphi: [*Strophe*

   In a valley shaded with fruit-trees, in the island of Delos,

   Leto gave birth to a lovely son and daughter:

     Apollo, the golden-haired musician,

     And Artemis, Queen of the deft bow.

   Then she took them from Delos, from the seaward valley

     Famed for their birth, and brought them

   To Mount Parnassus, mother of surging streams,

   Whose slopes ring with revels of Dionysus.

     There the dragon with wine-red eyes,

     With body of bronze and coloured scales,

   As fierce a monster as land or sea can show,

     Lay in the leafy laurel-shade,

   Guarding the ancient Oracle of the Earth.

       In your grip you seized him,

       New-born god Apollo,

   You, an infant dancing in your mother's lap, –

   Killed him, and possessed the holy oracle

       And the golden Tripod.

     Now from your sanctuary's chasm,

     Neighbour to the Castalian stream,

     Throne of infallible prophecy,

   You speak secrets of Heaven to mortal men,

   Lord of the central temple of all the earth!

     Now when Apollo came and drove   [*Antistrophe*

   Themis daughter of Earth from the sacred seat,

   Strange shapes stirred in the womb of the ground,

     And visiting dreams of night were born,

     And flew to the sleeping cities of men

   When darkness and deep rest had laid them still,

   And told them of things past and things to come.

     Thus ancient Earth, for her daughter's wrong,

     Took from Apollo his pride of place.

And Apollo leapt up and ran to Zeus on Olympus,
    Gripped the throne with his baby hand:
    'Father, rebuke the indignant Earth
Who steals my temple's honour with nightly visions!'
        And the Father, laughing
        At his child so eager
For men's worship, and the wealth of gold they bring,
Bowed his will that visions should no more reveal
        Word of gods to mortals.
    He took from men the elusive light,
    The half-remembered dark, of dreams;
    Restored to Apollo his prerogative
To answer throngs of suppliants from every city in Greece,
Chanting the high certainties of the will of Heaven.

Enter a MESSENGER.

MESSENGER: Guards! Attendants! [*He shouts, not to the* CHORUS, *but to those inside the temple.*] Where is the King? Where is Thoas? Open the temple doors and call the King out here!

CHORUS: If I may presume to speak – what is the matter?

MESSENGER: The two men have fled – gone! Iphigenia plotted their escape; and they've taken the holy image with them – it lies now in the hold of a Greek ship.

CHORUS: No! I can hardly believe you! But if you are looking for the King, he is not here; he has just left the temple hurriedly!

MESSENGER: Where was he going? I must tell him what has happened.

CHORUS: I don't know; but go after him, you will soon find him and be able to tell him!

MESSENGER: You women! I don't trust you! You're in the plot too, I've no doubt.

CHORUS: Are you mad? What have we to do with the men's escape? You'd better be off to your master's palace as fast as possible!

MESSENGER: Not until I get reliable information whether the King's in the temple or not. Hullo, there, in the temple! Draw the bolts! Tell the King there's a messenger here at the door with a load of bad news!

He hammers at the temple door, till it opens and THOAS
comes out, attended.

THOAS: Who is it raising this outcry in the very porch of Artemis, beating the door till the whole temple echoes?

MESSENGER: So! You were there all the time! These women were just telling me you had gone, and sending me off to look for you.

THOAS: Oh! What had they to gain by that? What are they after?

MESSENGER: I'll speak of them presently. The immediate business is, that the young woman who officiates here at the altar, Iphigenia, has gone — fled the country with the two strangers, and taken with her the holy image of Artemis! The purification was a trick.

THOAS: Iphigenia gone? What gave her the chance?

MESSENGER: This will surprise you more: it was to save Orestes!

THOAS: Who? Orestes? Clytemnestra's son?

MESSENGER: The victim Artemis consecrated here for death was Orestes!

THOAS: It is astonishing — more than astonishing! It is —

MESSENGER: Don't think of that now, but listen to me; and when I have put all the facts clearly before you, think out some plan for following them and hunting them down.

THOAS: Quite right: tell me everything. They have a long flight before them, if they hope to escape my sword!

MESSENGER: When we reached the shore, near the place where Orestes' ship had been secretly moored, Iphigenia turned to us guards, whom you sent to hold the prisoners, and motioned us to stand at a distance, so that she might light the holy flame and perform the purification. She took in her own hands the cord that bound the men, and walked behind them, alone. I admit that was suspicious; but your servants, my lord, thought there could be nothing wrong. After a while, to make us think she was still busy with the ceremony, she gave a loud cry, and began singing wild magical incantations, as if she were actually washing away the stains of blood. So time went on, and we were still sitting there; until it occurred to us that the men might get free, kill the priestess and run for it; but we still sat on in silence, for fear of seeing what is forbidden. However, at last we all agreed to go, in spite of orders, and look for them.

So we went; and there we saw a Greek ship, with her two rows of oars lifted, poised like a pair of wings! and fifty rowers at the ready, and the two young men, unbound and free, standing by the poop. Some of the crew were steadying the prow with poles, others were making the anchor fast to the cathead; and others again were hurriedly letting down rope-ladders to the sea, for the two Greeks to climb on board.

As soon as we saw this treachery, without any more scruple we ran and seized Iphigenia, caught hold of the cables, and tried to drag the steering-oar out of the socket; and we were shouting at them, asking what business they had to come stealing our statues and priestesses and sailing away with them. 'Who are you?' we cried, 'and where do you come from, to smuggle her off like this?' And the answer came, 'Let me tell you I am her brother Orestes, son of Agamemnon; and I am taking my long-lost sister home!'

We were still clinging to Iphigenia and trying to drag her off to you; but it cost us hard knocks and bruised faces, as you see. Neither we nor they had swords; but those two men came at us with fists and feet, and aimed such a volley of blows at us on every side, that to close with them was only to reel back beaten. They stamped their seal on every man of us; and we retreated, with broken heads and bleeding

eyes, to a spur of rock; and there we took our stand and
fought more cautiously, pelting them with stones. But we
were soon stopped: archers came up on the poop and drove
us back with a shower of arrows. At that moment a large
wave lifted the ship a little inshore; the foam swirled at
Iphigenia's feet, and she shrank back; Orestes raised her on
his left shoulder, strode into the sea, leapt at the ladder, and
set his sister safely inside the ship, together with the statue
of Artemis that fell from heaven.

Then from the body of the ship a voice shouted: 'Seamen
of Hellas, row! Churn the waves white! We risked the
Clashing Rocks and the Sullen Sea for this; and we have
what we came to get!' The crew replied with a triumphant
roar; the oars plunged; and the ship flew forward – but only
while she was in sheltered water. As she made out through
the narrows a choppy sea met her, and she was working
against the tide. Then a sharp wind sprang up suddenly and
began driving the ship back to land stern first. The men
heaved and fought, kicking against the current; and still the
running tide drove them in.

Then Iphigenia stood and prayed to Artemis: 'Daughter
of Leto, forgive my theft, and bring me your priestess safe
home to Hellas from this cruel country! Goddess, do you
not love your own brother? It is right that I should love
mine!' The sailors cried to Apollo to hear her prayer and
save them; they gripped the oars and strained their bare
arms in steady rhythm; yet still the ship came nearer, nearer
to the rocks. One of our men waded into the sea; another
tried to hitch a looped rope on to the ship. I left them and
came straight here to find you, my lord, and report what
has been happening there.

So get ropes and fetters and come at once! Unless the
swell dies down they have no chance of escape. The great
god Poseidon, Lord of the Sea, is Troy's protector and
enemy to the house of Pelops; and now, it seems, he intends

to hand Orestes over to you and our people, – and his sister,
who appears to have forgotten how Artemis saved her from
the knife at Aulis, and has turned traitor.

CHORUS: O Iphigenia, what will you do? If you and your
brother fall into the King's hands again it will mean death!

THOAS: Harness your horses, every man in the city, gallop to
the shore and be ready for the Greek ship when she grounds!
After the blasphemers with heaven's help and catch them!
Launch our fastest boats! We'll either take them at sea or
ride them down on land; then let us fling them from the
cliff, impale them on stakes! – You women! you were in
this plot: I shall punish you later at my leisure; just now I
have other things to do and can waste no time.

Several guards make off towards the shore.

Enter ATHENE; *she appears, a figure of superhuman size,*
above the porch of the temple.

ATHENE:

Wait, wait, King Thoas! What new prey is this
You hunt now? Listen to me: I am Athene!
Call back those armed men streaming in pursuit!

THOAS *signs to a guard, who runs.* THOAS *kneels.*

It was Apollo's word that sent Orestes,
Flying from the Furies' rage, here to this shore
To bring his sister home, and win release
From that relentless torment by conveying
Safe to my Attic soil the holy image.
That is my word to you. As for Poseidon,
He is not, as you think, rousing his waves
To engulf and kill Orestes, but already
Has calmed the sea's uproar at my request
And given a smooth path to Orestes' ship.
And you, Orestes – for my immortal voice,
Though far off, fills your ears – hear my commands:
Sail on with the holy emblem and your sister;
And, when you reach the god-built walls of Athens,

Right on the Attic boundary is a spot
Close to the Carystian Rock, a holy place
Called by my people Halae: you shall build
A sanctuary and set up the image there.
Name it the Taurian temple, to recall
This country, and your perilous exile
Driven by tormenting Furies from end to end
Of the Greek world; and there shall men henceforth
Raise solemn hymns to Taurian Artemis.
Give them this law: at every festival
The priest shall with his sword touch a man's throat
And draw one drop of blood, as ransom for
Your blood now spared, to give due reverence
And awe to Artemis. You, Iphigenia,
Shall serve her shrine at the Brauronian Steps
And hold her sacred keys. There, when you die,
They shall adorn your grave with braided gowns
Of softest weave, left in their store by women
Who die in childbirth.
                              Thoas: these women here
You must set free, and send them home to Greece:
This I command.
                              Orestes, when you stood
For trial in Athens, and the votes were even,
I cast my vote for mercy, and you live.
Let this be law for ever: when the votes
Are even, you shall spare and not condemn.
So, son of Agamemnon, carry home
Your sister; and you, Thoas, be content.

THOAS:

Divine Athene! To hear a god's command
And disobey, is madness. I renounce
All anger against Orestes and his sister
For the holy image they have taken from me.
No honour comes of measuring strength with gods.

Let them go safely on, and build a shrine
For Artemis, with Heaven's blessing, in your land.
These women too I will send home to Greece
And happiness, as you command. My ships
And warlike preparation, since your will,
Goddess, so stands, I cancel and recall.

ATHENE:

You are wise, for so you must. The gods themselves
Bow to Necessity. Blow, winds, and bear
Orestes on to Athens! I will go
With them, to keep watch on their holy treasure
In honour of my sister Artemis.

Exit.

CHORUS: Go, and good go with you,
              Rich in Fortune's favour,
              Numbered with the living!
        Great Athene, honoured by immortal gods,
              Held in awe by mortal men,
              We will do what you command.
        Past all wonder, now to our despairing ears
              Lips divine have spoken
              Words of joy and comfort!

ALCESTIS

*

Characters:

APOLLO
DEATH
CHORUS, *Citizens of Pherae in Thessaly*
FEMALE SERVANT
ALCESTIS, *wife of Admetus*
ADMETUS, *King of Pherae*
YOUNG SON *and* DAUGHTER *of Admetus*
HERACLES
PHERES, *father of Admetus*
MALE SERVANT

*

Scene: Before the palace of Admetus.

Enter APOLLO, *his bow slung over his shoulder, a quiver of
arrows at his side.*

APOLLO:
House of Admetus! Here I have submitted
To eat a labourer's bread, and be content –
Yes, I, Apollo, a god! The cause of this
Was Zeus, who killed Asclepius, my son,
Struck him with lightning to the heart. Then I,
Hot for revenge, killed Zeus's fire-makers,
The Cyclopes; for this, he sentenced me
To live in serfdom to a mortal man.
I came here to Admetus; until to-day
I have kept his herds, and brought luck to his house.
Finding my host worthy and god-fearing,
I saved his life, tricking the immortal Fates
To give consent Admetus should escape
Imminent death if he could find another

To take his place and join the dead below.
He asked in turn all of his family,
His father, and his mother; but found no one
Willing to quit this world and die for him –
Except his wife. She now is in the house,
Propped on their arms and gasping out her life.
For she must die: this is the day appointed
By Fate for her departure. And I too
Must leave this house, which I love dearly, lest
Its walls infect me with the taint of death.
Ah!
I see he is here already, – Death himself,
Priest of the dead. He has waited for this day;
Now he is punctual: he has come to take her
Down to the house of the dead, as Fate appoints.

Enter DEATH, *carrying a sword.*

DEATH:

Ah! Phoebus Apollo! Why are you here,
Still haunting this house,
To infringe, usurp, annul
The honours due to the Powers below?
Were you not satisfied
When with a clever trick you outwitted Fate
To cancel the death Admetus owed?
Now for Alcestis too
You come, armed with your bow,
Watching your chance to rescue her!
Did she not undertake
To forfeit her own life as the ransom due for his?

APOLLO: Be calm: I have right and reason on my side.

DEATH: Right, do you say? Then what are your weapons for?

APOLLO: It is my custom always to carry them.

DEATH: And to show unjust favours to this house.

APOLLO: Admetus is my friend. I share his griefs.

DEATH: So will you rob me of Alcestis too?

APOLLO: Admetus was not robbed from you by force.

DEATH: Then how comes he above ground, not below?

APOLLO: He has given you her, whom you have come to fetch.

DEATH: Whom I will fetch. She shall come down with me.

APOLLO: Take her. – And yet, I might perhaps persuade you –

DEATH: To kill those due to die? That is my work!

APOLLO: No! but to kill those who put off their time.

DEATH: I see your meaning, and your wish.

APOLLO: There is
         A way, then, for her to live out her life?

DEATH: None! I, like others, value privilege.

APOLLO: You receive one life only, young or old.

DEATH: But greater honour when the dead is young.

APOLLO: If she dies old, she will be richly buried.

DEATH: Phoebus, your law may favour wealth; not mine.
         You'd sell long life to the rich.

APOLLO: Do you say so?
         Your keen wit has gone long unrecognized!
         So, you'll not grant this?

DEATH: You should know me better.

APOLLO: I know you: hating men, hated by gods!

DEATH: There are some laws that even you can't break.

APOLLO:
    By heaven, you will yield yet, cruel as you are!
    A man to master you is on his way
    Now to this house, under Eurystheus' orders
    To bridle Diomede's wild chariot-horses
    And bring them back from the cold hills of Thrace.
    He will be kindly welcomed here; and he
    Will wrest Alcestis from your hand by force.
    You will do all that I have asked, and still
    Forfeit my gratitude and earn my hate.

                    Exit.

DEATH:

Yes, you have words enough: words win you nothing.
Now she shall come down to the dead. I'll go
And seek her with my sword, to celebrate
The fatal rite: when once this edge has severed
One lock of hair, that soul is sealed to me!

DEATH *goes into the palace. Enter the* CHORUS,
from the town.

CHORUS:

This is strange! No stir at the door,
No sound, but the whole house silent!
Not one friend of Admetus near to tell us
Whether our Queen, Alcestis, daughter of Pelias,
Is dead, and we must mourn her,
Or still lives in the light of day!
In my belief she is the noblest wife
A man ever had; and the whole city
Is thinking the same thought.

CHORUS A:

Do you hear any sound in the house   [*Strophe*
Of mourning or of weeping?
Any cry like the cry that breaks when all is over?

CHORUS B:

Not even a slave set to watch by the door!
O God of Health, bring respite,
And end this storm of troubles!

CHORUS A: There would not be this hush if she were dead.

CHORUS B: Ah, she is gone!

CHORUS A: They have not buried her yet.

CHORUS B: Why? I have little hope. What makes you sure?

CHORUS A:

It is not possible that Admetus
Should bury his true and noble wife
Privately, without calling friends to mourn her.

CHORUS A:

>When someone has died, it is customary   [*Antistrophe*
>To place a bowl of spring-water before the door;
>But I see none.

CHORUS B:

>And there would be a curl of hair hung here,
>Cut for a sign of sorrow, and the young women wailing,
>If she were dead.

CHORUS A: And yet this surely was to be the day –

CHORUS B: The day?

CHORUS A: When she must pass to the world below?

CHORUS B: The very thought is a wound to the soul!

CHORUS A:

>A noble life is all but spent;
>And a man must grieve whose heart
>The years have taught to be true.

CHORUS:

>If we sent by ship to the East,   [*Strophe*
>To Apollo's Lycian shrine,
>Or South to the thirsty sand
>Where the pillars of Ammon stand,
>Might there not come from the mouth of seer or priest
>Some word of help divine?
>Close gapes the gulf of the dead;
>There is no help left, no altar to supplicate
>Where the blood of a victim shed
>Might turn the hand of Fate!

>Yes, there was one whose skill   [*Antistrophe*
>Could lead Alcestis back
>From the door of death and the dark land:
>If Apollo's son lived in the day's light still!
>His touch raised up the dead,
>Till Zeus with the lightning's sulphurous crack
>Struck lifeless the healer's hand.

And now, where shall we turn, our last hope fled?

The King has left no pious act undone,
No prayer unsaid;
The altars every one
With blood of sacrifice are red;
And help or hope is none!

Enter a FEMALE SERVANT *of* ALCESTIS.

CHORUS: Look! Here's a servant coming out. She is weeping.
What will she have to tell us? Come, my girl; it's natural
that you should be distressed at your master's sorrow. Tell
us: is his wife still alive? or has she died?

SERVANT: What shall I tell you? Alive, yes; and dead too.

CHORUS: How can that be?

SERVANT: She can't hold up her head now. She is gasping for
breath.

CHORUS: Poor man! Such a good man, too, to lose such a
noble wife!

SERVANT: Noble she is, indeed; but Admetus is blind to
that. He will see the truth when he has lost her.

CHORUS: There is no more hope for her life?

SERVANT: No, her day has come. Time will not wait.

CHORUS: And suitable preparations are being made?

SERVANT: Yes; Admetus has ready the robes to bury with her.

CHORUS: Her death will make her famous, she may be sure
of that. She is by far the noblest woman that ever lived.

SERVANT: Truly she is; who will deny it? What must a
woman be, to surpass her? Could any wife give clearer proof
that she honours her husband than to die willingly in his
place? Well, the whole city knows that she is dying for him;
but it will touch your heart to hear how she has spent these
last hours in her home.

She knew that her appointed day had come; and first she
washed her white body in water from the stream; then she
went to her storeroom of cedar-wood, and took out a gown,

and jewels, and dressed herself becomingly; and she stood before the altar on the hearth, and prayed in these words to Hestia: 'Goddess, I am going below the earth; this is the last time I shall pray to you. Watch over my children. Give my son a loving wife, and my daughter a noble husband. Let them not be cut off in their youth, to die like their mother; give them good fortune and a long and happy life in their own country.'

She went to all the altars in the house, decking them with garlands of myrtle-leaves which she had picked herself, and praying. And all this time not a tear, not a sigh; there was no change in her lovely face, no paleness, nothing to show what was before her.

But then she went into her own room; and she threw herself on the bed, and wept a long time. 'Dear bed,' she cried, 'here I first gave myself to him; and now I die for him. Good-bye, my marriage-bed! I do not hate you; but you have been my death, you alone, since I refused to fail in a wife's duty. And now another wife will possess my place here. She may be happier: more true she could not be!'

My mistress knelt beside the bed and kissed it, her eyes streaming, till the coverlet was wet with tears. At last, when she could not weep any more, she went out, stumbling helplessly; but again and again after going out she went back and buried her face in the bed. Her children were holding her dress and crying; she took them in her arms and kissed them in turn and said good-bye to them. The servants everywhere were broken-hearted and weeping; she gave her hand to each one; they spoke to her, and she to them, even the most humble.

So: there is sorrow enough in Admetus' house. If he had died himself, – well, he would have died. Instead, he possesses a memory that will torment him as long as he lives.

CHORUS: This is surely a great distress to Admetus, that his loyal wife must be taken from him?

SERVANT: Oh, yes, he is weeping; clasping her lovingly,

begging her not to desert him. It is useless to ask that, when
she lies there, a limp weight in his arms, faint and sickening
to death. And now, though she is barely able to breathe, she
wants to take her last look at the sunlight. – I will go in and
say that you are here. It is not everyone who loves my master
enough to stand by him loyally in time of trouble; but I
know you are an old friend of the King's.

Exit to palace.

CHORUS A:

Zeus! Can we find no remedy, no way   [*Strophe*
To bring our master's house relief
From this inexorable Fate?

CHORUS B:

Ought we to wait
For news? Or has the moment come
For the shorn head and the black cloak of grief?

CHORUS:

The end is clear, too clear; yet we will pray
To the gods; for the power of gods is very great.
    Apollo, lord of healing,
    Show mercy to Admetus!
    Cheer him with hope unlooked for;
    Send now, send deliverance!
    As before you found a way to save,
    So again
    Break the chain of death to-day,
    And quell the cruelty of the devouring grave!

CHORUS A:

Weep for the King, cry and lament aloud,   [*Antistrophe*
Mourn for his bitter loss, his broken life!

CHORUS B:

Well might a man so cursed seek welcome death,
Quench his own breath with knife or noose hung high.

CHORUS:

For he this very day shall see his wife,

So dear, too dear for telling, now shall see her die!

> Look! Now the Queen is coming,
> And King Admetus with her!
> Lament, my land and city,
> Weep, O weep to see her go,
> Faint with death, in spirit loyal and brave,
> Steadfast to the gloom below,
> Into the earthy depth of the devouring grave!

> They say that marriage holds more joy than pain:
> I say such talk is vain!
> I judge from years past; and to-day I see
> Admetus struck by new calamity.
> When he shall lose his noble wife,
> Darkness thenceforth shall be his day, his life no life.

ALCESTIS, *supported by* ADMETUS, *comes from the palace; with
her, the little boy* EUMELUS *and his sister.* ALCESTIS *is at first
in a sort of trance or delirium.*

ALCESTIS:

> O Sun! O light of the day!
> O heavenward eddies of the scudding cloud!

ADMETUS: The sun sees what we both suffer, and can witness
that we have done the gods no wrong, to deserve your
death!

ALCESTIS:

> O Earth, and the walls of home!
> And Iolcus, where I lived as a girl in my father's house!

ADMETUS: Lift yourself up, Alcestis! Do not give in, but
pray! The gods are powerful, and may be merciful.

ALCESTIS:

> I see the two-oared boat coming over the lake;
> I see the ferryman of the dead,
> Charon, leaning on his pole;
> He is calling me now, 'Come, make haste, you delay me!'

You hear? He is urging me to come more quickly!

ADMETUS: You break my heart, Alcestis, when you talk of
Charon and his terrible boat – Oh! what are we to do?

ALCESTIS:

I feel a hand grasping my hand and leading me –
Do you see? Let me go, down to the house of the dead!
Death frowns at me; his eyes glow dark under his wings.
[*To* ADMETUS, *who clasps her.*] What are you doing? Let me
    go! As I follow
The way is dark and fearful, – oh, it is fearful!

ADMETUS: And we who love you are heartbroken; most of
all, I and these children who are weeping with me.

ALCESTIS [*the delirium is over*]:

Let go now; take away your hand;
Let me lie here.
I have not strength to stand;
And death is near.
Now darkness creeps over my eyes like night.
Children, my children, you have a mother no more,
No more! You will live in the sun's light.
Farewell!

ADMETUS:

O gods! To hear you say farewell
Is torture worse than death. I plead with you –
How can you bear to leave me, in God's name,
To leave your children? Courage! Rise and live!
How can I live when you are dead? For me
Living and dying are in you alone.
Your love claims more than love: I worship you!

ALCESTIS: Admetus, you see that I am dying. Before I go I
must tell you what my wishes are. I have chosen that you
should live rather than I, because I honour you as my husband. It would have been easy for me to refuse: as a widow
I could have married whom I chose in Thessaly, and been
rich, and ruled a king's palace. Instead, I am dying.

I did not want to live parted from you, and my children fatherless; and though I was young and happy, I have given up my youth and all its happiness. Your father and mother were of an age to die honoured by everyone; and to that honour they could have added the glory of saving their son. You were their only child, and they had no hope of another if you had died. Had they not failed you, we should have lived our length of years together. Instead, you are left alone to mourn for your wife and to bring up your children without a mother. But all this some divinity has ordained for us.

Your part, then, is to remember what I have done for you. Since life is a more costly gift than any other, I do not ask you for an equal return; but what I ask, you will allow, is just. You are a man, and love your children not less than I: keep them inheritors of my house; give them no stepmother to envy my royal birth and vent her jealousy in harshness towards your children and mine, Admetus! I beg you, do not do this! To children a stepmother comes in like an enemy, cruel as a viper! A boy has always a strong tower in his father; but what would be your fate, my daughter, what happiness would you find as you grew to womanhood, if your father took another wife? Might she not slander you in the flower of your youth to ruin your hope of marriage? Your own mother will never put on your bridal veil, nor hold your hand in childbirth, when her comfort is your deepest need. I must die. Not to-morrow, or after two days' grace, but this very hour I shall be spoken of as a woman who once lived.

Good-bye! Be happy! You may be proud, Admetus, that you chose a good wife; and you, my children, that you had a good mother.

CHORUS: You need not be afraid; I am ready to answer for Admetus. He is a good man; of course he will do as you wish.

ADMETUS: I will, I will! Never doubt me! You are my wife;

living or dying, you shall be always my only wife! No woman in Thessaly, however noble in birth, however beautiful, shall ever call me husband in your place. These children are enough for me; I pray the gods to give me joy in them, for my joy in you is lost.

I shall carry my grief for you not one year only, but as long as my life lasts. My father and mother are my enemies; I hate them. They say that they love me, and they will do nothing; but you bartered your own dear life for mine, and saved me. Now I am losing you: should I not mourn? There shall be no more dancing! The crowded feasts, the merrymaking that filled this house, the music – it is all ended ! I can never again take heart to touch my lyre, or sing to the Libyan flute: all pleasure dies with you!

I shall find a clever sculptor to carve your likeness, and it shall be laid on our bed, I shall kneel beside it and throw my arms round it and say your name, 'Alcestis, Alcestis!' and think that I hold my dear wife in my arms, snatching at cold comfort to ease the weight from my heart! Then in my dreams you would come to cheer me; it is a comfort to see a dear face even in a dream, for as long as the vision lasts.

If I had the song of Orpheus, music to beguile Pluto or Persephone, I would descend now and bring you back from the dead; Charon should not bar me, nor the watch-dog of hell, but I should raise you living to the light! ... It cannot be. Look for me there when I shall die. Wait for me, and make a home ready where we can be together. I shall command my children to lay my bones with yours, in the same coffin. You alone are true to me: I will not be parted from you even in death.

CHORUS: I am your friend, and share this deep sorrow with you. Alcestis is worth all your tears.

ALCESTIS: Children, you have heard for yourselves what your father promises: he will not marry and give you a second mother, but will honour me.

ADMETUS: I have given my word, and will keep it.

ALCESTIS: I believe you; and I entrust these children to you.

ADMETUS: Dear wife! Dear children! I take them from your hand.

ALCESTIS: You shall be their mother, now I am gone.

ADMETUS: I must, and will.

ALCESTIS: Children, I am going when you need me most.

ADMETUS: What shall I do without you?

ALCESTIS: Time will soften pain; and the dead – are nothing!

ADMETUS: Take me too, in God's name take me with you!

ALCESTIS: It is enough that I die for you.

ADMETUS: O gods! She is too good to die! Must I lose her?

ALCESTIS: My eyes are heavy. It is growing dark.

ADMETUS: You are leaving me – I cannot bear it!

ALCESTIS: I am already gone. I am nothing now.

ADMETUS: Look up! Will you leave your children?

ALCESTIS: I do not want to leave them. Children, good-bye!

ADMETUS: Look at them! Look at them!

ALCESTIS: I am gone.

ADMETUS: What is it? Are you faint?

ALCESTIS: Good-bye!

ADMETUS: Alcestis!

CHORUS: She is gone. Alcestis is dead.

EUMELUS:

> What shall we do? My mother
> Has gone into the darkness,
> And nowhere can we find her;
> She has left me to a lonely life!
> See! her eyes are shut now,
> And her hands are limp.
> Mother, listen! Listen to your little child,
> Calling you with kisses, kneeling by your pillow!

ADMETUS: She cannot hear or see you. Children, this blow is more than we can bear.

EUMELUS:

    I am young to walk alone
    Without her at my side.
    Who can tell what troubles this sad day has brought me,
    Which you must share, my sister?
    Father, why did you marry?
    Since she could not come with you to old age,
    But died and left you lonely;
    And with her our whole house is lost and dead!

CHORUS: Admetus, you must bear this sorrow. You cannot escape it. You are not the first of men, nor the last, to lose a noble wife. Consider: death is a debt that every one of us must pay.

ADMETUS: I know it. This was no sudden blow, nor was it mere chance. For a long time the foreknowledge of this day has tortured me. ... Now I must set in order her funeral rites. Stay with us, my friends, and chant a hymn to the implacable god of Death. I command every Thessalian in my dominions to do his part, and wear the shorn head and sombre dress of mourning for the Queen. Let all who drive chariots, and all riders, shear their horses' manes. Let no music either of flute or string be heard in the city, till twelve full months are past.

    I shall never carry to burial another so dear, nor so faithful to me. Her devotion claims every honour I can give; for she alone has given her life for mine.

    Servants now carry the body of ALCESTIS *into the palace.*
              ADMETUS *follows.*

CHORUS:

    Daughter of Pelias, may peace go with you   [*Strophe* 1
        To the unseen region
        Where your place awaits you
        In the sunless palace!
    Let the black-haired Lord of Death
        Know her well!

Let the ghostly ferryman,
   Aged Charon, crouching
   Over oar and rudder,
   Know his craft has carried
Deathwards over stagnant Acheron
   One alone the noblest
   Of all mortal women!

Many a poet shall make songs to praise you;   [*Antistrophe* 1
   Seven-stringed lyres shall voice them,
   Singers chant in chorus,
When the circling months bring round
Sparta's thronged Carneian feast,
While the full moon rides the sky all night;
   Or when shining Athens
   Fills **her** streets with singing:
   Such a theme for music
Has your death bequeathed to mortal minstrelsy!

   Would I had power to go   [*Strophe* 2
   Down to the River of Night,
To turn again that fatal oar,
   And bring you up once more
Away from the gloomy bounds where the waters of weeping
     flow,
   Into the day's light!
For you, beloved Alcestis, you alone,
To ransom from Death's bond your husband's life,
   Fearlessly gave your own.
Then lightly fall the earth to fill your grave!
If ever the King take another wife
  — (This I have sworn)
Mine and your children's hate and scorn
Shall persecute the man you died to save!

His mother's head was grey,   [*Antistrophe* 2
    His father's too; yet they,
With hard heart and averted face,
    Prized their last feeble breath,
And would not hide their flesh in its earthy bed
To save their own dear son from death.
But you in the fresh flower of youth
    Have taken Admetus' place,
    And now are dead.
    To win one such as she
    In tenderness and truth
To share my home and love – to gain
A blessing in this mortal world so rare –
    That would be my prayer!
With her my length of years would pass unclouded, free
    From every pain.

Enter HERACLES; *the* CHORUS *recognize him by his
        lion-skin cloak and his club.*

HERACLES: Tell me, good friends of Pherae, shall I find
    Admetus at home?

CHORUS: Admetus is at home, Heracles; but what is it you
    want? What brings you to Thessaly, and to Pherae?

HERACLES: I am engaged on a task for Eurystheus of Tiryns.

CHORUS: Where are you going? What remote journey is
    imposed on you now?

HERACLES: I am going to Thrace, to fetch Diomede's four
    chariot-horses.

CHORUS: What? But how can you? No doubt you know
    Diomede?

HERACLES: I do not. I was never in Thrace before.

CHORUS: You will not possess those horses without a
    fight. If you are to come back alive you will have to kill
    Diomede.

HERACLES: Well, to refuse the task is not in my power. It
    will not be the first time I have fought for my life.

CHORUS: And even when you have overcome him, what can you do then?

HERACLES: I shall bring back the horses to Eurystheus.

CHORUS: To bridle those beasts will be no easy matter!

HERACLES: I may succeed, – if they don't breathe flames from their nostrils!

CHORUS: Why, they attack men with their teeth and tear them in pieces!

HERACLES: Eat men? You're talking of bears and wolves, not horses!

CHORUS: You will see: their very mangers are wet with blood.

HERACLES: The man who bred them is the son of a famous father, is he not?

CHORUS: Yes, his father was Ares, lord of the golden Thracian shield.

HERACLES: You are right; and that too is part of my destiny – a rough, uphill road, every step. It seems I must fight all the sons of Ares in turn: first Lycaon, then Cycnus; and now I'm on my way to measure strength with Diomede and his horses. Well, I am Alcmene's son: no enemy shall ever see my hand tremble!

CHORUS: Ah! Here comes our king, Admetus, from the palace.

Enter ADMETUS, *with his hair cut in sign of mourning;*
a servant attends him.

ADMETUS: Heracles, son of Zeus and grandson of Perseus! Welcome!

HERACLES: Admetus, King of Thessaly! All happiness to you!

ADMETUS: So I could wish. . . . I know your thought is kind.

HERACLES: Why have you cut your hair? Are you mourning someone?

ADMETUS: I have a burial to perform to-day.

HERACLES: It is not one of your children? – God forbid!

ADMETUS: No; my children are well.

HERACLES: Perhaps your father? He was a ripe age.

ADMETUS: No, my father and mother are both alive.

HERACLES: It is not your wife Alcestis that has died?

ADMETUS: There are two answers I could give about her.

HERACLES: Do you mean she is dead or alive?

ADMETUS: She both is – and is no more. Hence my distress.

HERACLES: I am still no wiser. What do you mean?

ADMETUS: Do you not know what is fated to happen to her?

HERACLES: I know she undertook to die in your place.

ADMETUS: That once agreed, how can I say she is still alive?

HERACLES: Heavens, man! Don't start weeping for your wife so early. Wait till the time comes.

ADMETUS: Whoever must die – is dead; and the dead – are no more.

HERACLES: Most men see a difference between being alive and being dead!

ADMETUS: You think in one way, Heracles; I in another.

HERACLES: But who really has died? Why are you in mourning? Who is he?

ADMETUS: It is a woman I was speaking of.

HERACLES: Related to you?

ADMETUS: No; but a close friend of the family.

HERACLES: How came she to die here in your house?

ADMETUS: She came to live here when her father died.

HERACLES: Ah, well; I wish I had found you in happier circumstances, Admetus.

ADMETUS: What do you mean? Where are you going?

HERACLES: Why, to some other friend's house.

ADMETUS: My lord, I will not hear of it. I should be deeply hurt.

HERACLES: No guest is welcome on the day of a funeral.

ADMETUS: The dead – are dead. Now come indoors.

HERACLES: It is not right to sit and feast in a house of mourning!

ADMETUS: We will take you to the guest-rooms; they are in another part of the house.

HERACLES: I shall always be grateful to you; but let me go!

ADMETUS: I cannot allow you to go to another man's house. [*To the servant.*] Open the outer guest-rooms! Show him the way. Tell the stewards to provide an ample meal. And shut the courtyard doors – our guest at supper must not have his pleasure spoilt by sounds of mourning.

HERACLES, *followed by the servant, goes into the palace.*

CHORUS: Admetus! Have you the heart to entertain guests at a time like this? Are you mad?

ADMETUS: I am his host. If I had turned him from my house, or from my city, would you have praised me more? Far from it; that could not have made my position any less painful. I should have been guilty of discourtesy, my house called inhospitable, bad made worse. Besides, when I travel the thirsty roads of Argos, Heracles is always a generous host to me.

CHORUS: If he is your friend, as you say yourself, why, then, did you hide from him what has happened here?

ADMETUS: If he had known anything of the truth he would have refused to enter the house. There are some, no doubt, who will call me a fool for what I am doing, and blame me; but my house has yet to learn to shut the door in the face of a guest.

Exit ADMETUS *to the palace.*

CHORUS:

House of rich welcome and countless guests!   [*Strophe* 1
   House of the generous host!
   Here Apollo chose to live,
   The Soothsayer, the Musician,
And was content to keep the King's flocks,
   Piping a tune of shepherd's love
   Over the steep winding pastures.

Spotted lynxes loved his music and came   [*Antistrophe* 1
   To graze beside his flock;
   And a tawny herd of lions
   Came from the glen of Othrys;
   Apollo's lute rang clear,
And round him dappled fawns, stepping
Slender-footed from the high shady fir-trees,
Danced for joy to the god's enchanting notes.

   Thus for Apollo's sake   [*Strophe* 2
   Admetus' hearth and lands are blest
   With wealth beyond the rest
That live beside the pleasant Boebian lake.
Westward, his ploughed acres and level pastures lie
   Stretching to where the sun
Stables his horses on the gloomy plain
   Under the far Molossian sky;
While seaward, to the East, Mount Pelion,
On the rock-bound Aegean coast, is his domain.

Now again he has thrown open his door   [*Antistrophe* 2
And welcomed his guest, and has not told
   The cause of the tear undried,
While in the inner room the well-loved form
   Lies pale and cold
That but an hour ago was warm.
A kingly mind will honour to excess
   Duty and kindliness;
Yet in such folly, if the heart be true,
   Lies full wisdom too.
How this may be I cannot tell;
   Yet in my heart I keep
   Assurance rooted deep,
That he who fears the gods will prosper well.
Enter ADMETUS, *with attendants bearing the body of* ALCESTIS.

ADMETUS: Pheraeans, your presence here shows your friendly hearts. Everything now is ready; and attendants are carrying her shoulder-high to burial. Now, as she goes out on her last journey, will you pronounce for her the farewell that is customary?

CHORUS: Admetus, look! I see your aged father coming on foot, and servants with him, bringing gifts to offer to the powers below.

Enter PHERES, *attended.*

PHERES: My son, I have come to share in your sorrow. The wife you have lost was noble and chaste; no one can deny it. Suffering is hard; but we must learn to suffer. Accept these gifts, and let them be buried with her. It is our duty to honour her remains, for she has given her life for yours, my son. She would not let me lose you, or see me sink into a miserable and childless old age. She has shed a new dignity upon every living woman by her courageous and noble sacrifice. Farewell, Alcestis! You have saved my son, and raised me from the grave. Peace be with you, even in the house of death! – Listen, Admetus: with a woman like that, marriage pays; otherwise, it's a bad bargain.

ADMETUS: I did not invite you to this funeral; you are not here as one of my friends! Nor shall my wife wear any gift of yours – her grave will be honourably furnished without them. When I was ill and dying, that was the time for you to show your sympathy. Then you stood back; then you let another die, though you were old, and she was young. And after that you come to howl over her dead body! You are no true father of mine! You have been sifted, exposed for what you are – I refuse to be called your son! Surely you must be unsurpassed in cowardice! At your age, at the very end of your life, you had neither will nor courage to face death for the sake of your only son, but allowed her – a woman from another city – to die instead. She was father and mother in one person to me. Was it so great a sacrifice, set against the

glory of dying for your son? In any case you had only a short
time left to live; you had already enjoyed everything that a
man needs for happiness: the kingly power while you were
still young, a son to succeed you – so that there was no fear
of your house being left without inheritor to the rapacity of
strangers. – Or will you say it was because I dishonoured
your grey hairs that you left me to die? – I, who have
always given first duty and first reverence to you! And
with what gratitude you and my mother repaid me! I tell
you, you had better lose no more time in begetting children
to care for your old age, to shroud you and carry you to your
grave. I shall not lift a hand to bury you: for all you care, I
am dead! If I owe my life to-day to another's act of love,
that other, I say, claims the whole of my filial love and duty.
I have heard old men pray for death, abhorring the long slow
senile years: hypocrites! Let death but come within sight,
they decline to die! Old age has lost its terrors!

CHORUS: My son, Admetus, say no more. Is our present
trouble not enough? Do not goad your father to anger.

PHERES: Insolent boy! Whom do you think you are reviling?
Some wretched Lydian slave bought with your own money?
I am a Thessalian. My father was a Thessalian; we are of pure
blood and breeding, and well you know it. You go too far,
flinging your hot-headed insults; but you shall not turn your
back before I've answered you!

You are my son: I brought you up to inherit this palace;
but I am certainly not bound to die for you. There's no
tradition in Pherae that fathers die for their sons, – no, nor
in Hellas! Lucky or unlucky, your life is your own concern.
I have done my duty by you: you have wide possessions; I
shall leave you the large estate that I inherited; then what
have you to complain of? Have I robbed you? Don't die for
your father, and I'll not die for you. You enjoy life: do you
think I don't enjoy it? I expect to be dead for a long time,
and alive for a short time – yes, short, but still sweet. You

took pains enough, and without a blush, to avoid dying!
You have lived past your time, and killed her – yes, and
then you talk about my cowardice! You, a blackguard less
courageous than your own wife, who died to save her brave
young husband!

You are ingenious, too; you have hit on a way never to
die at all – get each successive wife to die for you! And then,
any relative of yours who declines, you abuse, being a
coward yourself! Now hold your tongue, and think this
over: if you love your life, why, so do all men; and your
insults to me will be repaid with interest, and with truth!

CHORUS: You have both abused each other more than
enough. Pheres, stop reviling your son!

ADMETUS: Talk on, I have said my say. If the truth hurts you
it is your doing; you are in the wrong.

PHERES: To die for you would have been still more wrong!

ADMETUS: Dying is different for an old man. I am young.

PHERES: A man has but one life to live – his own.

ADMETUS: Then I hope you may outlive Zeus!

PHERES: What have I done to earn such a curse?

ADMETUS: I thought you seemed in love with a long life.

PHERES: I? What of you? Aren't you burying her in your
place?

ADMETUS: Her tomb is a memorial to your cowardice.

PHERES: Oh! *I* killed her, did I? You say I killed her?

ADMETUS [*with a groan of exasperation*]: I hope you may need
my help one day!

PHERES: Marry wife after wife, let them all die for you!

ADMETUS: So they would – more shame to you for refusing!

PHERES: God gave us light; and it is sweet, very sweet.

ADMETUS: Whimpering weakness! Mockery of manhood!

PHERES: Mock me if you will; it's not *my* old body you're
burying.

ADMETUS: When you die you need expect no eulogies over
your grave.

PHERES: Little I care who slanders me – in my grave.

ADMETUS: Hear that! What sense of honour has an old man?

PHERES: *She* had honour. What she lacked was sanity – as you discovered.

ADMETUS: Leave me to bury her in peace; and go!

PHERES: I'll leave you: the murderer shall bury his victim. But you'll be brought to book yet by her family; if Acastus is the man he used to be he'll make you suffer for his sister's death!

ADMETUS: Get out of my sight, both you and your wife! Grow old childless as you deserve, though your son lives! Never come under one roof with me again! For my part, if it were lawful to proclaim publicly that I renounce a son's right in my father's hearth and home, I would have done so.

Exit PHERES. *There is a long silence, during which the waiting coffin is seen to be still at the centre of the stage.*

Now, my friends, we have a sad task before us, and must perform it. Let us go on to the place of burial.

CHORUS:

Farewell, Alcestis, fearless even to death,
High-hearted, first in faithfulness!
Hermes and the dread King
Give you kind welcome to the earthy shades!
If there high place is kept
For noble spirits, may you
Receive full honour, throned beside Persephone!

The CHORUS *join the funeral procession and exeunt. After the stage is empty, shouts and drunken singing begin to be audible inside the palace. The* SERVANT *who was ordered to attend* HERACLES *then enters.*

SERVANT: I have seen guests in plenty, and from all sorts of places, come to this house; and I've served them at dinner; but I never had a worse one than this. To begin with, he could see Admetus was in mourning; he ought never to

have crossed the doorstep; yet, in he walks. Then at table:
does he politely take what's put in front of him, seeing he
knows our circumstances? Not a bit! Anything we don't
bring, he shouts at us to fetch. He takes the ivy-wood cup
in his hands and tosses off the blessed liquor – neat! till the
drink goes to his head and begins to warm him up. He puts
on a wreath of myrtle-leaves and starts a hideous bawling.
Well, there were two tunes going on at the same time: he
was singing at table, not giving a thought to the distress
in the household; and in the servants' room we were all
weeping for our mistress. But we took care not to let
him see tears in our eyes; Admetus had given orders about
it.

And now, here am I indoors serving a guest – some
rascally thief or bandit; and Alcestis has gone; and I did not
follow her body; I could not even hold out a hand to say
good-bye, or join in the lament for my mistress. She was a
mother to me and to all the servants. A thousand times,
when the master was in a rage, she calmed him down and
saved us. This – guest, who comes bursting in on our
trouble, – I hate him, and with reason.

Enter HERACLES.

HERACLES: Here, you! Come here! Why do you look so
solemn? What are you cogitating about, eh? A servant ought
not to come scowling in front of a guest. You should be
affable, welcoming! Instead, you see before you an old
friend of your master's, – and you receive him with a
glowering face, as if you hated him! And all because you're
upset about your neighbour's troubles!

Come here! You're a man of understanding: I'll teach you
a little more understanding. Dost thou understand the
nature of mortal life? I don't think you do. How could you?
Well, listen to me. All men are inevitably bound to die.
There isn't a man in this world who can confidently say
whether he's going to live through the next day. For Fate

progresses in a mysterious way. The way of Fate no one can learn, neither is it to be grasped by skill of man.

Now: you have heard what I have to tell you; and you have understood it. Well, then, cheer up! Have a drink! Say to yourself, 'To-day my life's my own; to-morrow it belongs to Fortune.' And listen: there's nothing like love. The most charming, the most delightful of all divinities for a man to worship, is Aphrodite. Oh! she's a sweet, kind goddess, is Aphrodite! All these other cares and troubles, – forget them! and just do as I say, – if you realize that I'm giving you good advice, as I think you do.

Come along! Away with all this melancholy! Rise above circumstances! Put a garland on your head! And, my friend, join me in a cup of wine. That's the very medicine to cure your gloomy thoughts and scowling brow. The very sound of wine trickling into a cup will make a new man of you! You know, we're just mortal men, you and I; then why pretend to be anything else? As for these solemn souls with their knotted eyebrows, do you know what I think of them all? They aren't really alive! Life to them is one long disaster!

SERVANT: I know, I know; but to-day we are not disposed to merrymaking. We have other things to do.

HERACLES: Don't take it so much to heart; the poor woman was not of this family. Your master and mistress are well.

SERVANT: What? Well? Don't you know what has happened here?

HERACLES: Why, yes; unless your master lied to me.

SERVANT: He carries hospitality too far, much too far.

HERACLES: Must I be turned away for a stranger's funeral?

SERVANT: A stranger! If only it had been a stranger!

HERACLES: Is there some real trouble that he kept from me?

SERVANT: Please leave the troubles of this house to us.

HERACLES: This points to something more than a stranger's death.

SERVANT: It does; or why should I object to your enjoying yourself? It was not right to receive you at such a time.

HERACLES: But why should my friend treat me like this? Has he lost one of his children? or his father, maybe?

SERVANT: No, Heracles. He has lost his wife, Alcestis.

HERACLES: His wife! And you received me as a guest!

SERVANT: He was too honourable to turn you from the door.

HERACLES: Poor man! To lose Alcestis!

SERVANT: Yes; and we all feel that our life too has come to an end.

HERACLES: I saw his tears, and felt that grief lay deep under the outward signs. He said it was for a stranger's funeral; and I believed him, and blundered in, though reluctantly enough, to abuse the hospitality of a bereaved house with wine and feasting, and a garland on my head! And you – when this had happened, to tell me nothing of it! Where is he burying her? Where shall I find them?

SERVANT: As you leave the city, on the straight road to Larissa, you will see below you a tomb of polished stone.

Exit SERVANT.

HERACLES: Come, heart and hand, your endless endurance must be put to test! Now show what sort of son Alcmene of Tiryns bore to immortal Zeus! The woman's dead; and I must rescue her, and pay the debt of kindness I owe Admetus by setting Alcestis in her own home again – alive! ... The black-robed King of the Dead will come to drink the blood of victims offered at her tomb. That's where I'll find him: I'll hide there, watch for him, leap out and spring on him; once I have my arms locked round his writhing ribs, there's no power on earth shall wrench him free, till he gives her up to me! ... What if I miss my prey, if the bait of blood fails to fetch him? Then I'll go down to the sunless palace of Persephone and her King and ask for her; and, by my soul, I shall bring Alcestis up again and deliver her safe into Admetus' hands, – my true friend, who, sooner than send me away, even at a time of mortal sorrow, out of pure nobleness and love for me, hid his distress and received me as a guest in his house. Is there a heart more generous in Thessaly, in Hellas itself? He shall not say that his kindness was shown to an ungrateful friend.

    Exit HERACLES. *Enter* ADMETUS *and* CHORUS.

ADMETUS:

    O house ravaged and maimed!
    How can I cross your door?
    How can I see you without hate and dread,
    Anguish that will not cease?
    Earth has for me no way, no room.
    What can I say? All language is too poor!
    If only I were dead!
    A crushing fate has claimed
    My life from my mother's womb.

    How happy the dead are! Theirs is the peace,
    Theirs the dark home I envy and desire.
    The sunlight wakes no pleasure in my eyes,
    My foot treads the firm earth and feels no joy;
    So dear a life was pledged for mine,
    Till Death with a robber's hand
    Seized his unlawful prize
    And lodged her in the unseen land.

CHORUS:

    Pass on, Admetus; enter your sad home,
    Hide your head there!

ADMETUS:

    Have pity, friends!

CHORUS: Pity indeed is due
    To such deep anguish and despair.

ADMETUS:

    I am alone and desolate.

CHORUS: True;
    Yet of what use to her are all your tears?

ADMETUS:
    How can I cease?

CHORUS: Drink your full cup of pain:
    Not in all your years
    Shall you see Alcestis' face again.

ADMETUS:
    You touch my sick mind where the wound is deep.
    What sharper stroke can shatter a man's heart
    Than loss of his true wife?
    I should have lived a lonely man apart,
    Not brought her here to share my home and bed!

    I envy those who keep,
    Unmarried, childless, their sole strength
    To bear the griefs that one life's length
    Heaps on their aching head!
    When man can live secure
    From fears for child or wife,
    Why should he bear their sickness, why endure
    To see his marriage-bed despoiled of life?

CHORUS:
    Fate is upon you. You cannot wrestle with Fate.

ADMETUS: My fate!

CHORUS: Admetus, you
    Must surely set some limit to your despair!

ADMETUS: None to my sufferings!

CHORUS: They indeed are great;
    Yet you are not the first whose wife has died.
    Hand of Chance in different guise
    Heavy lies now here, now there:
    Learn to bear Fate's ordinance!

ADMETUS:

> What years of lonely mourning stretch ahead!
> Most noble! My place is at her side!
> You should have let me leap
> Into the deep grave and with her there lie dead!
> So Death would gain,
> Instead of one, two faithful souls
> Crossing the dread lake to the shadowy plain.

CHORUS:

> I had a kinsman lost a likely boy,
> His only son. Desolate, in the grey downward years,
> Yet he endured his sorrow patiently.

ADMETUS:

> My house! How can I enter, when you wear
> A look so strange,
> Your fortune fallen from its height?
> Between that day and this – O bitter change!
> I entered then by the dancing light
> Of Pelion's pine-torches, while the air
> Rang loud with wedding-songs; and her dear hand
> Was held in mine; a merry band
> Followed with shouts and blessed our happy state
> That joined two ancient noble families in one.
> To-day, impartial Fate
> Turns songs to mourning for the dead;
> My white-clad friends are gone:
> Black robes escort me homeward to my desolate bed!

CHORUS:

> This blow found you unskilled in suffering,
> Fed with good fortune. Yet your world, your life
> Are yours to-day: she has lost life and friends.
> This is not strange; death has divided many.

ADMETUS: Friends, that is true; yet I count her state happier than mine. No pain will ever touch her now; she has reached the end of life's troubles with a glorious name. But I have trespassed beyond my time; I should not be alive. Too late I know that my life will be a sorry thing. How shall I bear to go in and out of my palace? Shall I ever again give or receive a greeting at my door, and find pleasure in it? Where shall I turn? When I go in, the loneliness will drive me out; I shall see her empty bed; the chair she would sit in; in every room the dusty floor unsprinkled; the children stumbling around my knees, crying for their mother; and the servants lamenting the beloved mistress they will not see again – home will be intolerable!

If I go to the city, there will be weddings, banquets, companies of women – her friends, young like her: how can I face them? I must fly again. And behind my back enemies will whisper, 'There goes the man who did not dare to die, who has bought a coward's life with his own wife's death, who hates his parents for his own fault: is he a man?' I have capped my sorrow with a coward's name, – a blackguard, known for a blackguard. Friends, what have I to live for?

CHORUS:

I have searched through many books, [Strophe 1
I have studied the speculations of astronomers,
I have pursued innumerable arguments:
Yet I have found nothing stronger than Fate.
There is no remedy against Necessity,
Either in the Thracian inscriptions
Written down from the golden voice of Orpheus,
Or in all the salves and simples
That Apollo gave to the priests of Asclepius
To heal the many hurts of mankind.

Necessity alone has no altar, [Antistrophe 1
No image for men to propitiate,
Nor does she regard sacrifice.
May your hand, Goddess implacable,

In the coming years of my life never fall heavier
Than I have felt it in the past!
Even Zeus looks for your help
To perform what he ordains;
Steel cannot resist your strength;
In your absolute purpose there is no pity.

Fast in Fate's unyielding grip   [*Strophe* 2
    You are held; yet still endure!
Not by weeping will you raise the dead to life.
        Sons of gods immortal
        Wither into darkness!
    Dear in life Alcestis was;
    Dear in death she will remain.
        Noblest of all women
        Was your wife, Admetus!

Hers shall be no mortal's grave;   [*Antistrophe* 2
    Like a god's her monument
Shall be honoured, welcome pause for pilgrim's feet.
        Turning from the pathway
        Thus shall men pay worship:
    'For her husband's life she died;
    Now divine, undying, lives!
Gracious Spirit, hear and bless your worshippers!'
        So shall all revere her.

CHORUS: My lord, Admetus, look! Surely this is Heracles
    coming back to the palace!

Enter HERACLES. *His look is changed; sweat stands on his skin; his
    voice and bearing are those of one relaxed after unspeakable exer-
    tion. A veiled woman follows him.*

HERACLES: Admetus: to a friend a man should speak openly;
    if he feels his friend is to blame, it is better to say so. You
    were in trouble; and I think I might have been trusted to
    stand by you and show myself a friend. You never told me

that your wife lay dead in your house; but received and feasted me, saying your grief was due to a stranger's death. And there I sat with a garland on my head, spilling wine to the high gods, while you and all your house were in deep distress. You are to blame, my friend, you are much to blame for treating me in this way.

But I have no wish to add still further to your grief. Listen: I will tell you my reason for turning back to your palace. I am going now to kill Diomede, King of Thrace, and bring back his wild horses. Will you take this woman and keep her for me till I return? Should I prove unlucky — which the gods forbid! — I give her to you to serve in your house. She came into my hands after a hard struggle. I fell in with some Pheraeans who were arranging athletic contests, open to all comers, — well worth a strong man's muscle; and I won this woman, and have brought my prize here.

In the lesser events the prizes were horses; in the greater, the boxing and wrestling, a team of oxen, and the woman with them. It seemed wrong to let slip the chance of so fine a prize. So, as I said, you must take care of her for me. This was no robbery; she is paid for with my own sweat. Maybe the time will come when you will thank me.

ADMETUS: Heracles, in hiding my wife's death I did not mean to slight you or forget that you were my friend; but I had enough sorrow without the added grief of seeing you stride off straight from my door to stay with another man. As for this woman — I beg you, with all reverence, ask, if you can, some other Thessalian to receive her, — one who has not suffered. You have many friends in Pherae. Do not renew my sorrow. I should see her here, and weep — I could not help it. My heart is heavy enough already; do not add to the weight. There is no place here for a young woman, — at least she is dressed like a young woman. This is a man's house now; how could she live untouched as you would wish? My men are young: it is not easy, Heracles, to read

them rules. I speak for your own sake. – Or could she perhaps – no! Could I let her use Alcestis' room, sleep in her
bed? Two voices would cry reproach at me: one from the
city, 'He has betrayed the wife who saved him, flying to
another woman's arms'; and one from the grave, her voice –
I must reverence her; I must be very careful what I do.

– Whoever you are, young woman, you have the shape
and height of my dead wife; you stand like her. – O gods!
Take her away, Heracles, take her away! Why must you
torment me when I am helpless? As I look at her I see my
own Alcestis! My heart seethes, and my eyes flood! I begin
now to taste the full bitterness of my loss.

CHORUS: The chances of life stir no gratitude in me; yet they
are the gods' gift, and must be borne.

HERACLES: I wish I had strength enough to bring Alcestis
back from death to life, as a gift for you!

ADMETUS: I know your goodwill to me. But what help is
that? The dead cannot return to life.

HERACLES: Keep sorrow within bounds. Bear this with
patience.

ADMETUS: It is easier to give advice than to steel the heart.

HERACLES: If you wept for ever, what would you gain?

ADMETUS: I know; but I am crazed with a love of weeping.

HERACLES: It is love of those we have lost that makes us weep.

ADMETUS: I die for love of her; yes, even more than I can
tell you.

HERACLES: She is worth your love.

ADMETUS: I have no wish to live.

HERACLES: The wound is fresh now; but time will ease the
pain.

ADMETUS: Time? Yes, the same time that brings death to me.

HERACLES: You will want to marry again; a wife will heal
you.

ADMETUS: Be silent! I am surprised that you can say such a
thing to me. No woman shall ever share my bed again.

HERACLES: What? Not marry? Are you going to live a widower? Do you think that will do Alcestis any good?

ADMETUS: I must honour her, wherever she is.

HERACLES: You are right, most right; but you will be called a fool.

ADMETUS: I swear you shall never see me marry again! Heaven strike me dead, if I betray the dead!

HERACLES: I am glad that your love for your wife is steadfast. – Now be generous, and receive this woman into your house.

ADMETUS: No! no! I entreat you, by Zeus your father!

HERACLES: I tell you, it will be an error to refuse.

ADMETUS: But if I consent, remorse will gnaw my heart.

HERACLES: Consent! To be generous might yet bring you luck.

ADMETUS: You torture me! I wish you had never won her!

HERACLES: But, since I did, you share my victory.

ADMETUS: I know you speak from kindness. But she must go elsewhere.

HERACLES: If you say she must, she shall! – Are you sure you mean 'must'?

ADMETUS: She must – if – if you will not be angry with me!

HERACLES: I have good reason for begging so hard.

ADMETUS: Win, then! But what you are doing is hateful to me.

HERACLES: In time you will thank me; only do as I ask.

ADMETUS [to servants]: We must receive her; take her in.

HERACLES: I will not hand her over to servants.

ADMETUS: As you wish; take her indoors yourself.

HERACLES: No: I will give her only into your hands.

ADMETUS: I will not touch her; but – there is the house.

HERACLES: Your own right hand! Nothing else will satisfy me.

ADMETUS: My lord, I do not wish it. You are forcing me!

HERACLES: Come, your hand! Now, take her hand in yours.

ADMETUS [holding out his hand, and turning away]: I would as soon cut off the Gorgon's head.

HERACLES joins their hands.

HERACLES: You have her?

HERACLES draws the veil from her head;
ALCESTIS stands still and silent.

ADMETUS: Yes.

HERACLES: Then hold her for ever! And tell the son of Zeus he is a worthy and generous friend. Turn round! Look at her! Is she something like your wife? Now farewell tears, and welcome happiness!

ADMETUS: O God! O God! What ...? What can have happened? Is this my wife, Alcestis, her very self? Or is this joy some mockery sent by the gods to drive me mad?

HERACLES: It is no mockery. This is your wife.

ADMETUS: Surely it might be some unreal spirit from the grave –

HERACLES: You know me, Admetus; I'm no necromancer!

ADMETUS: I saw her die: is this truly my wife?

HERACLES: Even so. Little wonder that you shrink from believing it.

ADMETUS: My wife – alive! May I touch her? May I speak to her?

HERACLES: Speak to her. Your utmost wish is fulfilled.

ADMETUS: Dearest! It is your face, your body – it is you! I thought you were lost for ever; now you are mine again.

HERACLES: Yes, she is yours. And may the gods bear you no envy!

ADMETUS: Great son of greatest Zeus! May he who begot you prosper and keep you all your days! You have saved me from despair, you alone. All blessing on you! How did you bring her up from the world of darkness?

HERACLES: She was under Death's authority. I fought with Death.

ADMETUS: But where did your fight with Death take place?

HERACLES: Near the very tomb. I took him unawares and closed with him.

ADMETUS: Tell me, why does she stand here not speaking a word?

HERACLES: She is still consecrated to the gods below. For three days, until she is purified, you may not hear her voice. Come, take her in. And pay your debt to me, Admetus, by showing your guests henceforth a true respect. Now I must go; I have work to do – Eurystheus is my master. Good-bye!

ADMETUS: Stay with us! Join in our feast and thanksgiving!

HERACLES: When I come back. But now I must lose no time.

ADMETUS: Good luck go with you, and bring you safe home!

Exit HERACLES.

ADMETUS: I command our citizens and all the land to celebrate this joyful deliverance with dance and festival! Let every altar run with fat of sacrifice! – Our life is changed: a new and better day now rises. I confess that Fortune has been kind to me.

CHORUS:

> Gods manifest themselves in many forms,
> Bring many matters to surprising ends;
> The things we thought would happen do not happen;
> Things unexpected God makes possible:
> And that is what has happened here to-day?

NOTES

(These notes have been kept as few and as brief as possible. In general, I have not included information which can be more satisfactorily found in a small Classical Dictionary.)

*

HIPPOLYTUS

P. 27 *The Cyprian*: the Greek name 'Aphrodite' is native to Homeric verse and fits awkwardly into iambics; so that 'Kupris', 'The Cyprian', is almost everywhere used in tragedy. (This name, in fact, frequently drops its personal meaning and becomes an abstract noun for 'sexual love'.) In the translation I have kept 'Aphrodite' throughout for the sake of clarity.

The Amazon: the Queen of the Amazons, Hippolyta, captured in war by Theseus. Shakespeare in *A Midsummer Night's Dream* makes her Theseus' honoured bride; but in the original legend she was a virgin queen subdued by force to the bed of her conqueror. Euripides plainly has this less happy situation in mind as the psychological background of the character of Hippolytus.

P. 31 *To me she is nothing at all*: the Greek phrase is an ironically polite dismissal, 'Many good-byes to her!' This blasphemy is unconsciously echoed by Theseus on p. 58, in reference to divination by means of birds. As there seems to be no suitable ironic phrase in English to fit both passages, I have used a plain and flat statement.

P. 37 *O my mother!* Phaedra was the daughter of Pasiphaë, who gave birth to the monster called the Minotaur. For this sense of hereditary guilt compare Theseus' words on p. 52, 'Far from here this harvest grew', etc.

P. 38 *The Queen's pitiful cry*: this may refer to Phaedra's words, 'It is he, the Amazon's son!' But presumably during the Nurse's speech Phaedra would be audibly weeping.

P. 39 *And life offers us many pleasures*: here follow four lines which I have ventured to omit. Their meaning is as follows: '... many pleasures: long gossipings and idleness, a pleasant evil; and the sense of shame. Now there are two qualities called "sense of shame"; the one is not evil [i.e. probably, conscience, which deters men from evil]; the other is a curse to families [i.e. shameful deeds]. If these two different qualities were clearly and aptly named, they would not be represented by the same letters.'

There are several passages in other plays where Euripides refers to 'gossip' as a thing likely to corrupt women (e.g. Andromache in *The Women of Troy*; see the other volume of Euripides in this series, p. 104). There are also passages where he makes a character discuss the meaning of some word. Both kinds of passage were noted as characteristic of him, and no doubt often parodied. Here, in the middle of Phaedra's agonized confession, such banal irrelevance seems to me to go beyond anything found elsewhere in Euripides, and I therefore regard these lines as possibly or probably spurious.

P. 42 *Of your saying any word about me:* the question how far Phaedra understands the Nurse, whether she tries to deceive herself or remains innocent in intention, is purposely left ambiguous by Euripides, who thus achieves an effect far more dramatic than that of a clear decision either way.

P. 43 *Love, the child of Zeus:* Eros.

P. 44 *You are beside the door:* the door is, of course, at the back of the stage; the Chorus are in the *Orchestra*, below and in front of the stage.

P. 51 *A solemn mission of piety:* Theseus has been enquiring formally from an oracle (probably that of Delphi) whether his expiation is now complete (see p. 28, 'His hands stained with the blood of the Pallantides'), and has, ironically enough, returned assured of the favour of Heaven.

That is all I know, Theseus: it was a dramatic convention that the Chorus must keep secrets entrusted to them. For them to tell at this point all that they know would be to prevent the tragedy. They are provided with an excuse for their silence by Phaedra's solemn charge to them before her last exit. Their failure to save Hippolytus by telling Theseus the truth has often been quoted as an instance of Euripides' failure to reconcile his matter with his medium. But in actual production no difficulty is felt here, because it is plain to the audience that the Chorus are partly outside the action of the plot.

Besides, if Hippolytus will not break his oath, why should the Troezenian women?

P. 56   *Take Orpheus for your lord and prophet:* there seems to be no evidence for any connexion between Hippolytus and Orphism; neither does Hippolytus' remark on p. 31 ('A loaded table's a cheerful sight after hunting'), nor indeed his occupation as a hunter, suggest that he was a vegetarian. Rather Euripides presents Theseus as a middle-aged man who is ready enough to regard fancy cults as responsible for lack of principle in the younger generation – by no means an out-of-date characteristic of middle-aged man.

P. 58   *To me they are nothing at all:* see p. 31, note.

P. 59   *My unhappy mother:* the fact that it is this remark which rouses Theseus to a climax of fury gives another strong hint of the tangled emotional relationship implied by Euripides as existing between Theseus and his son. Euripides is following his usual practice of making heroic characters think and feel like fifth-century Athenians. It is noticeable that Theseus realizes he has lost control, quickly recovers himself, and goes out on a rather lame threat.

P. 62   *You have proved a true father to me:* this is the second time (see p. 54) that Theseus has claimed Poseidon for his father; but Artemis twice (pp. 65 and 70) reminds him firmly that his father was the mortal Aegeus, though in her second speech she refers to the giver of the three curses as 'your father'.

P. 66   *I never would have submitted to such dishonour:* the impregnable callousness of this and other remarks of Artemis (especially, 'My own hand shall strike down', etc., p. 69) convey Euripides' emphatic valuation of the comforts of religion. Man in extremity must look to himself alone.

P. 71   *When was man more noble?* it is generally supposed that these words carried a reference to Pericles, who died the year before this play was produced.

IPHIGENIA IN TAURIS

P. 73   *Euripus:* the long narrow strait between the island of Euboea and the Greek mainland.

P. 74   *Calchas:* a priest and seer who accompanied the Greek Army
        throughout the Trojan war, who on several occasions declared
        that the gods required human sacrifice.
        '*Thoas*' means 'swift'. This remark of Iphigenia's has no ap-
        parent significance in the play, unless we take it for another
        instance of the curiously personal relationship between
        Iphigenia and Thoas which is hinted at on p. 110.

P. 76   *O Apollo!* Orestes had been brought up at Delphi, the centre
        of worship of Apollo. His murder of Clytemnestra, com-
        manded by the Delphic oracle, was regarded by Aeschylus and
        Sophocles as just and inevitable, though disastrous. Euripides
        in this and other plays, notably *Electra*, treats Orestes' act of
        revenge for his father as a piece of plain wickedness charac-
        teristic of the Apolline priesthood, and showing its natural
        effect in the mental and spiritual degradation of Orestes, who
        in this play at least is shown as a man more to be pitied than
        blamed.

P. 77   *The Unfriendly Sea:* the Greek name for the Black Sea was
        'Euxeinos', 'hospitable'. This euphemism was originally not
        merely tactful nor ironic, but apprehensive and propitiatory.
        I therefore translate it by its opposite, which best conveys the
        feeling of the name. The word 'axeinos', 'unfriendly', is itself
        frequently applied to the 'Euxine' Sea, e.g., near the opening
        of the Chorus on p. 85.

        Euripides' geography in this play is more than vague and
        quite inconsistent. Though Crimea is a very long way from the
        Bosphorus, near which the Clashing Rocks were supposed to
        be, he sometimes makes his characters speak as if the distance
        were only a few miles; e.g., Iphigenia's promise on p. 96 to
        send Pylades safely beyond the Purple Rocks – surely some-
        what more than she could answer for.
        Eurotas: the river of Sparta.

P. 79   *That first wickedness:* the quarrel between Atreus and his
        brother Thyestes over a lamb with a golden fleece (not to be
        confused with the golden fleece brought by Jason from
        Colchis), which culminated in the fatal 'banquet of Thyestes',
        at which Thyestes unwittingly ate the flesh of his own children
        served up to him by Atreus.

Swerved from his course: for the notion that the Sun was polluted by beholding an act of wickedness, see also p. 110.

Leda's daughter: Clytemnestra was the sister of Helen.

P. 80   *Symplegades:* the 'Clashing' Rocks.

P. 85   *Dirce:* the river of Thebes.

P. 91   *The letter was written for me:* this curious assumption that neither Iphigenia nor any of her Greek attendants could write has never been satisfactorily explained. If Phaedra could write, why not Iphigenia?

P. 100 *Oh, I am helpless!* This is an utterance almost of despair, certainly of desperate urgency. It is curious to note how, a few lines further on, Iphigenia seems to have forgotten the imminent danger, and to be ready to spend a long time in exchanging news with Orestes, instead of planning escape. Does Iphigenia possibly share to some degree her brother's mental instability? Probably the explanations on p. 101 are necessary to emphasize the tragic nature of the whole story (see the Introduction). It has been suggested that Orestes' account of the personal appearance of the Eldest of the Furies and the two Olympian deities in the Court of Areopagus – in such obvious contrast to the rationalism of the Herdsman – marks the beginning of another fit of madness.

P. 102 *I appeared before the Court of Areopagus:* This famous trial, for which the Court of Areopagus was said to have been founded, is the subject of *The Eumenides*, the third play of Aeschylus' Oresteian trilogy.

P. 104 *It would be wrong:* to us this may seem a foolish and unconvincing scruple; but to a Greek the unwritten law binding host and guest, the law of 'xenia', was very far-reaching and a basic principle of morality and of piety. This is well illustrated in *Alcestis*.

P. 106 *Remember those that you have loved:* the Chorus have already remembered them (p. 91). The embarrassing selfishness of Iphigenia, pointed as it is by Thoas' final threat to the Chorus (p. 117), strongly marks the heroic character of the women of the Chorus, and ensures their place in the dramatic pattern: they are not colourless onlookers, but the only entirely admirable people in the play.

Shapely laurel of Delos: what is known in the play of the characters of Apollo and Artemis does not affect the tender pathos of these memories of the happiness and beauty associated with festive worship at the great temples.

P.112 *This is the story of the oracle of Apollo at Delphi:* this first line is my own insertion. It seems necessary in English to make clear at once the connexion of this ironical Ode with the part given to Apollo throughout the play.

Visiting dreams: the third emphatic reference in this play to the significance of dreams. When we recall that this play was written during the period following the first arrival of news of the Sicilian disaster, it becomes plain how poignantly this story of dreams and disappointments, of bereavement and reunion, must have affected its first audience.

P.114 *When I have put all the facts clearly before you:* the situation described by this Messenger at the end of his speech indicates that his errand to Thoas is urgent; yet he takes time to spread himself over his account of what has happened. This inconsistency is allowed by the Greek dramatic convention, and will be found to justify itself in production if the actor playing the Messenger is reasonably competent.

P.117 *Poseidon:* the god of the Sea.

P.119 At the end of the play the MSS add three lines apparently intended to be spoken by or on behalf of the poet, appealing to Nike, 'Victory', to grant him the prize awarded for the best play:

> Holy, mighty Victory,
> Watch my ways and keep my life,
> Give me still the poet's crown!

ALCESTIS

P.121 *Tricking the immortal Fates:* the legend said that he made them drunk with wine and extracted the bargain from them before they recovered.

Imminent death: presumably from some common ailment. After the 'bail' was arranged, Admetus ascertained by enquiring of the Delphic oracle on what day Death would claim his right under the bargain.

P.133 *What shall we do?* In these two speeches of Eumelus the text is fragmentary and the matter frigid. They are included here for the sake of completeness, but any modern producer would surely cut them.

P.136 *That would be my prayer:* in the MSS the Chorus are called 'elders' of Pherae; but this utterance suggests the appropriateness of including at least one younger man among them.

P.137 *If they don't breathe flames from their nostrils:* Euripides seems to take some pleasure in puzzling us as to Heracles' real thoughts. This line and the two following certainly ridicule the legend of the fire-breathing horses; yet the reference to 'all the sons of Ares' sounds serious enough. This mystery is essential to the role here assigned to Heracles, who, though a necessary part of the story, remains outside its intimate circle. We do not know him; he arrives from nowhere and departs into mystery. The result is to isolate the one thing about him that matters: his relationship to Admetus, and the lesson he has to teach him.

P.140 *He who fears the gods:* this means, the man who respects hospitality. A failure in hospitality was an offence against Zeus. This line, then, is a hint of the play's dénouement.

P.144 *For my part, if it were lawful ...:* a good example of the Greek instinct to avoid ending a speech on a climactic note. This deliberate climbing-down is so foreign to our dramatic sense that many producers would feel justified in cutting this last sentence.

The departure of the funeral procession makes a good moment for an Interval. After the Interval the shouts and singing from behind an empty stage suitably introduce the new scene.

P.145 *Dost thou understand ...?* Heracles in his drunken pomposity uses an archaic form instead of the usual word for 'do you know?' But he can't keep it up, and relapses at once into 'I don't think you do'. In the same way, a line or two further on, Euripides gives Heracles four consecutive lines with trisyllabic rhyming endings; this effective feature of alcoholic rhetoric is to some degree reproduced in the words *say ... day ... way.*

A second volume of
Euripides' plays containing
THE BACCHAE, HELEN, ION, *and*
THE TROJAN WOMEN
and also translated by Philip Vellacott
is in active preparation
for this series

SOPHOCLES

THE THEBAN PLAYS

Translated by E. F. Watling

L 3

'The translator is not only a good scholar but also a sensitive producer and actor, so that the theatrical values are much clearer than usual. The dignity of the great orchestra-theatre is maintained, yet the lines will come easily from the lips of a modern and the plays are revealed as containing many unexpected twists of character and even of humour. . . . A trilogy eminently playable.' – E. Martin Browne in *Drama*

'Mr Watling's translation of the dialogue into a "much resolved" form of iambic line and the choruses into rhyming verse is extremely successful; its great beauty and extreme speakability far outweigh the few mistakes. Mr Watling has interesting things to say in his introduction about the plays themselves, his methods of translation, and the problems of production.' – *Journal of Hellenic Studies*

'Mr Watling is to be congratulated not only on the lucidity and sound scholarship of the translation, but on his success in enabling the reader to grasp the character of these great dramas and the atmosphere in which they were first enacted.' – *Sheffield Telegraph*

TACITUS

THE ANNALS OF IMPERIAL ROME

Translated by Michael Grant

L 60

Tacitus tells a story so vividly that he is often referred to as if he were a visual artist, for instance Racine called him 'the greatest painter of antiquity'. He is also one of the greatest historians who have ever lived. His short historical monographs *On Britain and Germany* have already been translated for the Penguin Classics; this is a new version of the last and most important work of his maturity, the *Annals*. It is easily the best source of information about imperial Rome during a period of momentous significance for the future – from the last months of the life of Augustus to the last years of Nero. As at no other time, the entire Mediterranean region, a world in its complexity, was a single political unit and its advanced Graeco-Roman civilization, described by Tacitus with all its merits and faults, has left many traces which survive even to-day. Superimposed on the whole enormous structure, superimposed, too, upon a Republican constitution, was one man, the emperor; and Tacitus shows us, in detail, the results which came from the domination of successive autocrats, men of strange and formidable personality. The spectacular events in the capital are of permanent value for the light they throw on the workings of power and influence, and on a great state's varying attitudes to problems of loyalty.